Rising Damp

A comedy

Eric Chappell

A SAMUEL FRENCH ACTING EDITION

SAMUELFRENCH.COM
SAMUELFRENCH-LONDON.CO.UK

ISBN 978 0 573 11376 5

www.SamuelFrench.com
www.SamuelFrench-London.co.uk

FOR PRODUCTION ENQUIRIES

UNITED STATES AND CANADA
Info@SamuelFrench.com
1-866-598-8449

UNITED KINGDOM AND EUROPE
Plays@SamuelFrench-London.co.uk
020-7255-4302

Each title is subject to availability from Samuel French, depending upon country of performance. Please be aware that RISING DAMP may not be licensed by Samuel French in your territory. Professional and amateur producers should contact the nearest Samuel French office or licensing partner to verify availability.

First produced as *THE BANANA BOX* in June 1971, at the Phoenix Theatre, Leicester directed by Stephen MacDonald. The character Rooksby subsequently became Rigsby. The character Noel Parker subsequently became Alan. The cast was as follows:

ROOKSBY . . . . Wilfrid Brambell
NOEL PARKER . . . . Keith Drinkel
PHILIP SMITH . . . . Neville Aurelius
RUTH JONES . . . . Janet Michael
LUCY . . . . Louise Nelson

Subsequently transferred to the Apollo Theatre, London, in June 1973 with the following cast.

ROOKSBY . . . . Leonard Rossiter
NOEL PARKER . . . . Paul Jones
PHILIP SMITH . . . . Don Warrington
RUTH JONES . . . . Frances de la Tour
LUCY . . . . Louise Nelson

The version of the play printed here was revived for a national tour in 2013 by Classic Comedy Productions and directed by Don Warrington with the following cast:

RIGSBY . . . . Stephen Chapman
ALAN . . . . Paul Morse
PHILIP SMITH . . . . Cornelius Macarthy
RUTH JONES . . . . Amanda Hadingue

CHARACTERS

RIGSBY, landlord, mid-40s.
ALAN, a fresh-faced young man in his early 20s.
PHILIP, a young black man.
RUTH, late 20s, tall and gangly but attractive.

SETTING

The interior of an attic flat.

TIME

Late-1960s.

ACT ONE

(The interior of an attic flat. An autumn evening in the mid-sixties. There are two rooms. The larger room which is the sitting room takes up most of the set.)

(The smaller room, upstage left and on a higher level, is the bedroom. There are two single beds visible through the cutaway wall. There is a suitcase by one of the beds.)

(A door, facing stage right, leads from sitting room to bedroom. The sitting room is sparsely furnished with second hand furniture. There is a fireplace with a gas fire stage right.)

(A wrinkled carpet and a dingy three-piece suite are downstage centre. Upstage centre are two windows overlooking rooftops. Cupboards and gas rings stand by the windows.)

(A door, upstage right, leads to the landing and stairs. A large wardrobe stands right of the door facing downstage.)

(RIGSBY and ALAN enter.)

(RIGSBY is a man in his mid-forties. He has a grim, ravaged face and is drawing on a cigarette. ALAN is a fresh faced young man in his early twenties. He is carrying a suitcase.)

RIGSBY. Well, here it is…

(ALAN puts down his case and looks around.)

ALAN. It seems bigger – bigger than when I came with my father.

RIGSBY. That's because I've decorated in pale colours – it broadens a room – gives a sense of space.

(He looks around the room with evident satisfaction.
ALAN *stares in vain for signs of recent decoration.)*

What you have here is an attic flat which is functional...
(points to gas rings) ...but with just a hint of luxury.

(He pats the back of the settee fondly.)

What was he in?

ALAN. What?

RIGSBY. Your father?

ALAN. In?

RIGSBY. During the war?

ALAN. Oh. The RAF.

RIGSBY. *(sniggers)* A Brylcreem boy.

ALAN. He's bald.

RIGSBY. *(darkly)* That was the excessive use of hair lotion.

*(ALAN *looks around.)*

ALAN. I know what it is. Some of the furniture's gone.

RIGSBY. No, it hasn't.

*(ALAN *examines the carpet.)*

ALAN. There was a table just here. You can still see the
marks.

RIGSBY. That table didn't belong here.

ALAN. Where is it now?

RIGSBY. Downstairs. The man downstairs has got it.

ALAN. That's not fair. I took the room with a table.

RIGSBY. Don't get on to me. I'm doing the college a favour
squeezing you in.

ALAN. You didn't say anything about squeezing me in when
I came with my father. You made us a cup of tea.

RIGSBY. What did he think of it, your father?

ALAN. He thought it was high up.

RIGSBY. *(snorts)* He would. That's typical. Typical of
the RAF. Most of them couldn't stand heights. You

couldn't get half of them up a ladder. How we won the war I'll never know.

ALAN. What about the Battle of Britain?

(RIGSBY *crosses to the window.*)

RIGSBY. I'm not denying it's high up. It is high up. I'm insured against low flying aircraft. It's in the policy. There's nothing between this room and the Urals.

ALAN. *(stares)* Are you sure?

RIGSBY. Of course I'm sure. There's nothing between this house and Russia.

(*He looks out broodingly.*)

This is the way they'll come...

ALAN. Who?

RIGSBY. The Russians. What else did he say, your father?

ALAN. He said he'd liked to have met Mrs Rigsby.

(RIGSBY *is silent for a moment.*)

RIGSBY. We were on parade with them in Manchester.

ALAN. Who.

RIGSBY. The RAF. They couldn't march to save their lives.

ALAN. Does that matter with the RAF?

RIGSBY. Of course it matters. They were a spectacle. There were five hundred of them and they didn't make a sound. Do you know what they were wearing? *(shakes head)* Rubber boots.

(ALAN *bends to examine gas rings.*)

Watch the gas! It kicks back. If it starts hissing like a snake don't try and light it – leave the door open and fetch me. *(pause)* And one other thing. The bathroom's on the next floor. It's a bit of a way but make the effort. Don't go filling things up in here.

ALAN. *(shocked)* I wouldn't dream of it.

RIGSBY. That's all right then. But I had one fellow up in here – he was a medical student too. The things I found. *(darkly)* He was responsible for the hole...

ALAN. The hole?

(**RIGSBY** *nods towards the carpet.*)

RIGSBY. Under the carpet. Miss Jones was removing her clothes one night – finished up covered in plaster. He had his eye to that hole in the floor, no doubt completing his study of anatomy. I moved him on after that.

(*He studies* **ALAN** *for a moment.*)

I suppose you've heard of the permissive society?

ALAN. Well, yes.

RIGSBY. It stops at that front door.

ALAN. That won't worry me. I'm here to study.

RIGSBY. That's what they all say – at first.

(**ALAN** *crosses to the wall by the window and runs his finger down it.*)

What's the matter?

ALAN. There's water running down the wall.

RIGSBY. What did you expect – champagne?

ALAN. Is the room damp?

RIGSBY. No. He says it's damp but it's not.

ALAN. Who does?

RIGSBY. How can you have rising damp up here? We're miles above sea level. It's healthy – like Switzerland. It's not damp.

ALAN. Then what is it?

RIGSBY. Condensation. Because he will try and cook a five course meal on two gas rings. You can't see across this room some nights. It's not my fault his suits are turning green. I told him.

ALAN. Told who? Who are you talking about, Mr Rigsby?

RIGSBY. (*hesitates*) Your roommate.

ALAN. What roommate?

(**ALAN** *enters the bedroom for the first time. He sees the two beds and the suitcase. Turns.*)

Wait a minute. There was only one bed here when I came with my father.

RIGSBY. Was there?

ALAN. Yes.

RIGSBY. Well, there's been a bit of a mix-up.

ALAN. I'll say there has. I took this room on the understanding that I wouldn't have to share.

RIGSBY. Look, I didn't expect him to come back. I didn't want him back. It's not as if I made him welcome. But he rolled in this afternoon as large as life. And I've had to assemble another bed.

ALAN. *(nervously)* Why didn't you want him to come back?

RIGSBY. There's something about him. He makes the hair on the back of my neck curl. Ever had that feeling?

ALAN. Yes – I'm getting it now.

(He moves towards his suitcase. RIGSBY follows him.)

RIGSBY. I wouldn't have had him last year but Miss Jones recommended him. She's in the offices. I didn't like to refuse.

ALAN. Well, that's not my problem.

(ALAN picks up his suitcase. RIGSBY detains him.)

RIGSBY. This doesn't suit me either but I don't seem to be able to discourage him.

ALAN. Why should you want to discourage him?

RIGSBY. You'll see...

ALAN. I won't because I'm leaving. I'm not sharing a room with anyone.

(RIGSBY regards him for a moment.)

RIGSBY. You're not a bedwetter, are you?

ALAN. *(indignantly)* No!

RIGSBY. Just thought I'd ask. Anyway, where could you go tonight – at this hour?

ALAN. *(hesitates)* I don't know.

RIGSBY. Look at it this way. He probably won't want to share with you – in which case it would solve both our problems. Just spread your stuff around...

(*He takes* ALAN*'s case and crosses back to the bedroom. He puts the case on a bed and starts to unpack for him. He takes out a bible and prayer book. He regards* ALAN.)

Bible. Prayer book. Church goer?

ALAN. (*uneasily*) My mother put them in.

RIGSBY. Wise thought. You'll need them. You'll need all your faith around here.

(ALAN *looks down at the abandoned suitcase.*)

ALAN. What's he like?

RIGSBY. Calls himself Smith but I don't think that's his real name.

ALAN. (*appalled*) You don't mean he uses an assumed name?

RIGSBY. I wouldn't put it past him.

(RIGSBY *takes out* ALAN*'s clothes.*)

Take up as much space as you can. He hasn't unpacked yet.

ALAN. I don't like to.

RIGSBY. You've got to stand your ground.

ALAN. I don't mind standing my ground but I don't want to take his.

RIGSBY. He'd do it to you.

(*He places the bible and prayer book prominently on bedside table.*)

We'll leave these where he can see them – bound to put him off.

(*He places* ALAN*'s striped pyjamas on the bed. Examines them.*)

Thick cotton. Good. You'll need them up here. He wears next to nothing and then complains about the cold.

ALAN. (*alarmed*) What?

RIGSBY. That's right. Spread your stuff around. Crowd him out. That's what you've got to do...

(*He crosses with* ALAN*'s suit and hangs it in the wardrobe by the outer door.* PHILIP, *a young black man, enters from the landing. He is casually but expensively dressed. He is handsome, regal, a little older than* ALAN. *He stares at them in well-bred surprise.*)

(ALAN, *who has followed* RIGSBY *out of the bedroom, gapes in astonishment.* PHILIP *regards* ALAN *for a moment and then turns to* RIGSBY.)

PHILIP. What's he doing here?

RIGSBY. Moving in.

PHILIP. He's not. I took this room as a single. I'm not sharing.

RIGSBY. Ah, that's the dilemma.

PHILIP. What dilemma?

RIGSBY. He says exactly the same thing. He says he won't share with you at any price.

ALAN. (*alarmed*) I didn't say that.

RIGSBY. That was my understanding.

ALAN. I didn't think there'd be enough room.

PHILIP. There isn't.

RIGSBY. I don't know what you two are complaining about. When I was in the army there was thirty of us to a hut not much bigger than this – and we never complained. (*pause*) Mind you, we were of the same ethnic background...

PHILIP. (*sharply*) What is that supposed to mean?

RIGSBY. Just that there's bound to be tension...under the circumstances..

PHILIP. What circumstances?

RIGSBY. Different outlooks...alien cultures...

ALAN. That's nothing to do with it. I didn't know that...
(*stops*)

PHILIP. What? What didn't you know?

ALAN. *(pause)* That I was expected to share.

PHILIP. Neither did I.

RIGSBY. *(soothingly to* PHILIP*)* Look, I'm in a difficult position. There's been a misunderstanding. I didn't expect you back. It's not as if you've been happy here. It's always been too cold for you – coming, as you do, from warmer climes. See, you haven't even unpacked your suitcase. That shows an obvious reluctance to stay. *(slyly)* I wouldn't be surprised if you hadn't been out looking for somewhere better...

PHILIP. That wouldn't be difficult to find.

RIGSBY. *(sharply)* Then why stay?

PHILIP. Because it suits me to stay.

RIGSBY. Ah, but does it suit him?

ALAN. Yes.

RIGSBY. *(surprised)* What?

ALAN. Now I look around I can see there's plenty of room. I'd like you to stay.

PHILIP. *(coldly)* This is my place and you'd like me to stay? Where have I come across that attitude before?

ALAN. *(hastily)* I didn't mean it like that.

PHILIP. Let's get one thing straight – this is my room and you don't invite me to stay.

ALAN. No.

PHILIP. *(pause)* But since it's late, and you've nowhere to go, I'm inviting you to stay.

ALAN. Thank you.

PHILIP. And that's my bed.

ALAN. Sorry.

(He moves his things to the other bed. RIGSBY *rolls his eyes.)*

By the way, have you eaten?

PHILIP. No.

ALAN. That's a pity.

PHILIP. Why?

ALAN. No table.

PHILIP. What!

(PHILIP returns to the living room.)

I thought there was something missing. Where is it?

ALAN. The man downstairs has got it.

PHILIP. That table belongs here.

ALAN. That's what I said.

RIGSBY. No, it doesn't. The table belongs downstairs.

PHILIP. Rigsby, I took this flat fully furnished...

(He takes a towel and washing things from his case.)

...without a table it's not fully furnished. You're in breach of our agreement. I expect that table to be returned...

(He exits.)

RIGSBY. Did you hear that? He's more chance of being struck by lightning. *(uneasily)* I suppose he'll tell Miss Jones. She always takes his part.

ALAN. Well, I can see his point of view.

RIGSBY. Oh, can you? I must say you turned out to be a real Naafi candle. I thought you didn't want to share?

ALAN. Yes, but when I said that I didn't realise he was... *(hesitates)*

RIGSBY. What?

ALAN. You know...

RIGSBY. What?

ALAN. *(lowers voice)* Black.

RIGSBY. *(dryly)* Oh, you noticed that, did you? Well, perhaps you noticed something else – I didn't mention it. The word never passed my lips. I have to be careful – and there's Miss Jones to consider. She's a great believer in good causes.

ALAN. I don't mind sharing.

RIGSBY. Good. I'm glad you take that view because if there's any trouble – you'll be the first to go.

ALAN. Why?

RIGSBY. Because he's a member of an under-privileged minority – and you're not. And there'll be trouble. He's always complaining. I wouldn't mind but he's never known luxury like it. He never had a pair of shoes on until he came here.

ALAN. I can't believe that!

RIGSBY. You watch him. You can see they're pinching his feet. He'll have them off as soon as he can. They have to feel the ground under their toes.

ALAN. No, they don't – they're no different from us.

RIGSBY. All right – if they're no different from us – why do they always break down on the M1?

ALAN. *(stares)* I didn't know that they did.

RIGSBY. Haven't you seen them standing on the hard shoulder – staring with childlike bewilderment at their steaming radiators?

ALAN. No.

RIGSBY. Well, I have. Mind you, don't mention any of this to Miss Jones.

ALAN. I don't even know her...

(**RIGSBY** *regards him doubtfully.*)

RIGSBY. Are you sure? She's in admin. Deals with student accommodation. Sure you haven't met her?

ALAN. No.

(He continues to regard **ALAN** *suspiciously.)*

RIGSBY. Not a woman you'd easily forget.

ALAN. Really?

RIGSBY. She's a friend of mine but I'm not rushing it. You know what I mean?

ALAN. I think so.

RIGSBY. She's got a wonderful pair.

ALAN. Has she?

RIGSBY. That's because she's untapped. There's a lot of pent-up force in there. One day she'll burst like a dam – and I'll be waiting. *(sharply)* All right with you?

ALAN. *(hastily)* Yes.

RIGSBY. *(brooding)* She hasn't replaced herself, you see. That's a law of nature – it's in all of us. You deny it at your peril.

ALAN. Have you replaced yourself, Mr Rigsby?

RIGSBY. No. Sad, really, to think I've no one to leave all this to.

(He gestures around the squalid room. ALAN looks around doubtfully.)

The trouble is I can never get her on her own these days.

(RIGSBY *scowls in the direction of the landing.)*

ALAN. *(smiles)* I suppose that's important if you want to replace yourself.

(RIGSBY *fails to spot the irony.)*

RIGSBY. It's essential.

(RIGSBY *exits.* ALAN *continues unpacking, pausing occasionally to glance towards the carpet in the middle of the room. Finally he crosses and scuffs the carpet with the back of his foot. He bends down and peers at the floorboards.* PHILIP *enters.)*

PHILIP. Looking for something?

(ALAN *hurriedly straightens the carpet.)*

ALAN. This damned carpet – almost tripped over it.

(PHILIP *throws his toilet bag down.)*

PHILIP. Well, the bathroom hasn't changed. There was a ring round the bath and one dirty towel.

ALAN. Does he provide towels?

PHILIP. When you've been here a few days you'll look back and laugh at that remark.

ALAN. He doesn't.

(ALAN *takes out a towel.*)

PHILIP. He doesn't provide anything but he sometimes removes things.

ALAN. Like the table.

PHILIP. And the bath plug.

ALAN. What?

PHILIP. If he feels there's been a run on the hot water.

ALAN. What do you do?

PHILIP. I have my own.

(*He hands* ALAN *a bath plug.*)

ALAN. Thanks.

(PHILIP *crosses and sits in the easy chair. He eases off his shoes and stretches his toes.* ALAN *stares.* PHILIP *catches his eye.*)

PHILIP. Is something the matter?

ALAN. *(hastily)* No.

PHILIP. Could you pass those Oxfords – in the wardrobe?

(ALAN *takes an expensive pair of shoes from the wardrobe and passes them to* PHILIP *with a smile. He watches* PHILIP *slip them on.*)

ALAN. Do you like England?

PHILIP. It's all right.

ALAN. What do you like best?

PHILIP. *(considers)* The telephone boxes – they're rather nice.

ALAN. Is that all?

PHILIP. And that the wild animals are in zoos...

(*He glances towards the landing.*)

Well, with a few exceptions...

ALAN. Do you get many wild animals?

PHILIP. There is more water than land in my country – and more crocodiles than people.

ALAN. Crocodiles! Do they attack you?

PHILIP. Yes.

ALAN. What do you do?

PHILIP. You wrestle with them.

ALAN. I couldn't do that.

PHILIP. But I'm the son of a chief. I'm not allowed to show fear.

ALAN. *(impressed)* I thought there was something different about you.

PHILIP. *(smiles)* I sensed that.

ALAN. Smith can't be your real name.

PHILIP. No. My real name is known only to the elders. You see, my people believe that when a man has your name he can do you harm. That he can take your name and work evil with it. Besides, it's far too long and you'd never be able to pronounce it. It means, he-who-must-be-obeyed-but-whose-name-must-never-be-uttered-except-in-council. You can imagine how long that takes to say.

(He slips on a jacket.)

ALAN. Going out?

PHILIP. Yes, thought I'd go for a Chinese meal.

ALAN. Well, I haven't eaten – perhaps I could –

PHILIP. I'm meeting someone.

ALAN. Oh.

(PHILIP studies him.)

PHILIP. This is rather awkward.

ALAN. Is it?

PHILIP. I may bring a girl back.

ALAN. Here?

PHILIP. Yes.

ALAN. All night?

PHILIP. Possibly.

ALAN. What about me?

PHILIP. *(smiles)* I'm afraid you'll have to find your own.

ALAN. I didn't mean –

PHILIP. Wait a minute – that's an idea. Suppose I was to bring one back for you?

ALAN. *(hurriedly)* No. Not on my first night. What would Mr Rigsby think? He says the permissive society stops at the front door.

PHILIP. He may think that but it's not true.

ALAN. Suppose he finds out?

PHILIP. He won't. I move silently – he never hears me. But I hear him. *(smiles)* You see, nature has a way of compensating a primitive people. There's a movement in my body that warns me of the approach of strangers.

ALAN. Mr Rigsby's not a stranger.

PHILIP. Believe me, there's no one stranger than Rigsby. I feel his presence as I feel the wind as it ruffles the hair of the springbok on the far side of the hill.

ALAN. But that won't stop him coming up. And there's no key to that door. What do we do then?

(PHILIP smiles. He takes a chair and wedges against the door.)

That doesn't look very secure.

PHILIP. That's merely to impede his progress. In the meantime...

(He removes the chair, crosses, opens the wardrobe door and ushers an imaginary person inside. He closes the door.)

ALAN. I don't think that's a good idea. Miss Jones is in the room below. Suppose she complains?

PHILIP. She won't.

(PHILIP picks up the bible and glances at it.)

You don't have any other objections, do you?

ALAN. No. I just don't think it's a good idea.

PHILIP. It's not a question of it being a good idea – as far as I'm concerned it's a necessity.

ALAN. Is it?

PHILIP. I left ten wives in my country.

ALAN. What?

PHILIP. I miss them. Because of that I find it difficult to sleep alone.

ALAN. Ten wives! You're not old enough.

PHILIP. We mature early in my country.

ALAN. When were you first married?

PHILIP. On my fourteenth birthday – it was part of my initiation.

ALAN. (gasps) On your fourteenth birthday? All I got was a bike! Ten wives – don't you find that a bit intimidating?

(PHILIP pauses by the door.)

PHILIP. Not really – it's rather like driving in traffic – you only see the one in front...

(PHILIP exits. ALAN shakes his head in wonderment. He opens the wardrobe door and bows an imaginary person in. He glances once more at the carpet. He crosses and bends over it. RIGSBY enters.)

RIGSBY. What are you looking for?

ALAN. (straightens) The top off my pen.

RIGSBY. (looks around) Where is he?

ALAN. Gone for a Chinese meal.

RIGSBY. He's not bringing it back here.

ALAN. He's going to the restaurant.

(RIGSBY crosses and looks out the window.)

RIGSBY. Restaurant. I signed a petition but it didn't stop them. You know what that place is, don't you? The end of the opium trail.

ALAN. You think so?

RIGSBY. They're all in the pay of Chairman Mao.

ALAN. Surely not.

RIGSBY. Agents of Red China – dedicated to the overthrow of Western Society – rotting its fabric from within.

ALAN. *(smiles)* With Chinese food?

RIGSBY. With opium. Then they'll be ready to take over. You can smile. Do you know what they believe? That when God made us – he put us all in the oven. We were taken out too soon – they were done to a turn – and friend out there was cooked to a frazzle.

ALAN. I think he's meeting a girl.

RIGSBY. That's something else he's not bringing back here. I'm not having Miss Jones tormented by creaking bed springs.

ALAN. I'm sure that doesn't concern me.

RIGSBY. It concerns him though, doesn't it?

(He makes for the door.)

ALAN. Well, you can understand it. He does have ten wives.

(RIGSBY *turns in astonishment.)*

RIGSBY. Ten wives! Bloody hell!

(he recovers himself.)

Well, marriage doesn't mean the same to them, does it. They get married every time there's a hurricane – when they think God's angry with them.

ALAN. No – it was expected of him. He's the son of a chief.

RIGSBY. *(stares)* Son of a chief?

ALAN. He's an important man in his country.

RIGSBY. Important. *(looks around)* What's he doing here?

ALAN. *(slyly)* I suppose this place was selected.

RIGSBY. *(impressed)* Do you think so?

ALAN. They needed somewhere convenient – close to the college – with a warm friendly atmosphere – functional with just a hint of luxury.

RIGSBY. I suppose you're right. Why does he call himself Smith?

ALAN. His real name's taboo.

RIGSBY. Then why doesn't he say my name's Taboo? Instead of being so bloody secretive?

ALAN. No – I mean his name can't be spoken – it's known only to the elders. But I think there's another reason. There's probably a power struggle in his country – there usually is. The Foreign Office probably advised him to keep a low profile.

RIGSBY. Foreign Office...

(He crosses thoughtfully to the door. turns.)

Revolutionaries. Envy, that's what it is. They probably noticed his mud hut's bigger than all the other mud huts... *(Pauses. Thoughtfully)* Specially selected?

(RIGSBY exits. ALAN smiles. He crosses to the door and listens. There is the sound of an argument off. Noises on the stair. ALAN's smile broadens. He opens the door. RIGSBY struggles in with a table.)

Where do you want this?

ALAN. Over there.

(RIGSBY places the table in the middle of the room. ALAN stares at the surface.)

What's that? Blood?

RIGSBY. *(peers)* No. Tomato sauce.

ALAN. He wasn't eating off it!

RIGSBY. Who?

ALAN. The man downstairs?

RIGSBY. I told him I might need it at any time. Do you know what he was doing? Sandwiching his peas. Talk about embarrassing, they all drummed down on the lino. And he's manager of the Co-op Drapery.

(He gives ALAN a searching glance.)

You certainly find people out when you live with them...

(He exits.)

(Lights fade.)

(Curtain.)

Scene Two

(ALAN *is in a dressing gown. He is sitting at the table reading a book.* PHILIP *enters. He frowns slightly at the sight of* ALAN.)

PHILIP. I thought you'd be in bed.

ALAN. Haven't you noticed anything?

PHILIP. What?

ALAN. The table's back.

PHILIP. Oh, yes. So he had a change of heart.

ALAN. No. *(proudly)* I got it back. I told him you were the son of a chief.

PHILIP. I wish you hadn't done that.

ALAN. He was impressed. I told him this dump had been specially selected and he believed me. *(Pause. Curiously)* Why did you come here?

PHILIP. *(shrugs)* It was convenient – and Miss Jones recommended it. I didn't want to disappoint her. Since she lived here I could hardly say it wasn't good enough.

ALAN. That was very sensitive of you.

PHILIP. Does that surprise you?

ALAN. What?

PHILIP. That I'm sensitive.

ALAN. No.

(PHILIP *picks up one of* ALAN's *books.*)

PHILIP. What are you taking?

ALAN. Medicine.

PHILIP. That could be useful. We get pneumonia once a fortnight around here.

ALAN. Actually, I'm more interested in research. *(solemnly)* The secret of life.

PHILIP. Really?

ALAN. The mystery of the living cell. Do you know what I'd like to prove?

PHILIP. What?

ALAN. That God exists – scientifically.

(PHILIP *suppresses a smile.*)

PHILIP. Scientifically. That should please him.

ALAN. What are you doing?

PHILIP. Town and Country Planning.

(ALAN *suppresses a smile in turn.*)

You find that amusing?

ALAN. Well, it hardly goes with the jungle.

(PHILIP *regards him seriously.*)

PHILIP. Do you know what I intend to do with the jungle?

ALAN. No.

PHILIP. Tarmac it.

ALAN. *(stares)* Tarmac the jungle?

PHILIP. The worst parts. What do you think?

ALAN. *(cautiously)* I've never thought about it. It's an interesting idea.

PHILIP. Think of it. Where once there was only the mosquito there would be trees growing out of black velvet tarmac. Lions would pad silently under fluorescent street lights. There'd be motorways and traffic lights and zebra crossings...

(Silence.)

ALAN. You're putting me on.

PHILIP. Yes.

ALAN. You've got quite a sense of humour.

PHILIP. Does that surprise you?

ALAN. No.

PHILIP. Well, I'm going to bed.

ALAN. No girl.

PHILIP. What?

ALAN. You didn't bring a girl back.

PHILIP. I'd almost persuaded her. We'd reached the end of the road when Bleak House loomed out of the shadows and she suddenly remembered a previous appointment. I could hardly blame her.

(**PHILIP** *throws off his jacket.*)

Aren't you going to bed?

ALAN. Yes. *(awkwardly)* I've got these ridiculous pyjamas...

PHILIP. Have you?

ALAN. My mother packed them. Striped. I look like a stick of rock.

PHILIP. I never wear them.

ALAN. *(alarmed)* Don't you?

(**PHILIP** *switches off main lights. He takes off his shirt aware that* **ALAN** *is watching him. He puts on long African-style night shirt. He bends to remove his trousers.*)

ALAN. Are you circumcised?

(**PHILIP** *straightens.*)

PHILIP. Oh, my God!

ALAN. I just wondered. Are you?

PHILIP. Yes.

ALAN. So am I. *(pause)* Rotten, isn't it?

PHILIP. You should have it done when you're twelve – in the bush – with a blunt knife.

ALAN. Oh. Does it hurt?

PHILIP. It does make your eyes water a little.

ALAN. I suppose it's more hygienic.

PHILIP. That's what they say. They're mad about it in my country. They even do the girls.

ALAN. Crikey. *(pause)* How do they do the girls?

PHILIP. Aren't you going to get some sleep?

(**PHILIP** *gets into bed.*)

ALAN. In a minute.

(He crosses to the window and checks outside.)

PHILIP. *(sighs)* What are you doing now?

ALAN. Just checking to see how we'd get out if there was a fire.

PHILIP. Do you often do that?

ALAN. First thing I do when I'm anywhere new. It's a long drop...

(He turns back.)

Have you met Mrs Rigsby?

PHILIP. No.

ALAN. I understood he was married.

PHILIP. I've never seen her.

ALAN. Don't you think that's strange?

PHILIP. I haven't thought about it.

(ALAN looks about the room.)

ALAN. You don't think she's walled up somewhere? Standing behind the wallpaper – staring at us?

PHILIP. It's possible. But I'm not going to spend the night worrying about it.

(PHILIP switches off his bedside light. Only ALAN's small light illuminates the room. ALAN crosses to his bed. He hesitates and then crouches down.)

PHILIP. *(curiously)* What are you doing?

ALAN. *(muffled)* Nothing.

PHILIP. You're supposed to do that downstairs.

ALAN. I'm not doing that!

(PHILIP sits up and switches on his light.)

PHILIP. Then what is it? Oh no! You're not praying.

ALAN. Yes.

PHILIP. Are you going to do that every night?

ALAN. I was going to do it in bed but I don't think it's the same, do you?

PHILIP. I don't see that it makes any difference.

ALAN. I think it has more significance if you get out in the cold. And I'm also bearing witness.

PHILIP. *(sharply)* Not for my benefit, I hope.

ALAN. Well, no –

PHILIP. You're not doing any missionary work around here. Don't try and convert me. There's no point.

ALAN. Why?

PHILIP. Because I happen to be a god, that's why.

(ALAN stares at him in astonishment.)

ALAN. You're joking.

PHILIP. No.

ALAN. But that's ridiculous.

PHILIP. My people don't think it's ridiculous. They believe I'm a god. A god of earth – of light – of fire. The trouble with you Christians is you only believe in things you can't touch. When you come across the reality – it frightens you.

ALAN. I'm not frightened. I just don't believe you.

PHILIP. Then I'll prove it. I'll work a miracle.

ALAN. What sort of miracle?

PHILIP. *(smiles)* I'll make something appear…

(He takes something that looks like a war club from the cupboard. ALAN shrinks back. PHILIP switches off the lights and crosses to sitting room. He taps three times on the floor. He waits. Silence.)

ALAN. Nothing's happening.

PHILIP. Sh!

(ALAN switches his bedside light on.)

No. Don't switch on the light!

(ALAN switches off the light.)

It's coming. I hear it. I feel its presence…

(There is the sound of steps on the stair. The door from the landing opens letting in a shaft of light. **RUTH JONES** *enters, a shadowy figure in a night dress.)*

(She stumbles across the floor and collides with the furniture.)

RUTH. Blast! *(low voice)* I'm here. Damn! You could at least put a light on. Where are you? You know I can't see you in the dark.

(She enters the bedroom.)

You're teasing me again, aren't you...?

(There is the sound of a scuffle in the bedroom followed by a loud crash. **PHILIP** *switches on the lights.)*

*(***ALAN** *and* **RUTH** *are sprawled out on the wreckage of his bed.* **PHILIP** *watches them with a sardonic smile from the living room.* **ALAN** *stares at* **RUTH** *in astonishment.* **RUTH** *is in her late twenties. She is attractive in a tall, gawky way but there is a faint primness around her mouth.)*

(She returns **ALAN**'s *look of surprise.)*

RUTH. What are you doing here? Have you missed your train?

ALAN. No.

PHILIP. He's sharing the flat.

ALAN. *(tired of being anonymous)* My name's Alan.

PHILIP. Alan's sharing the flat.

*(***RUTH** *pulls her negligee closer about her.)*

RUTH. He can't. There won't be enough room.

PHILIP. That's what I said. Alan, this is Ruth.

RUTH. Hello. I'm sorry if I was abrupt. I didn't realise. *(pause)* Are you all right for sugar?

ALAN. Yes, thank you.

RUTH. Mr Rigsby didn't say anything about this.

PHILIP. I suppose he saw the chance of doubling the rent. He knew you wouldn't approve.

RUTH. I don't. Never mind, Alan. I'll find you somewhere better in the morning.

ALAN. That's all right – I like it here.

(**RUTH** *and* **PHILIP** *exchange glances.*)

RUTH. Are you sure?

ALAN. Yes.

RUTH. But your bed's collapsed.

ALAN. I'll fix it.

RUTH. Oh. Then I'd better go – that crash must have woken the house. He mustn't find me here...

(She exits cautiously. **ALAN** *looks incredulously at* **PHILIP**.*)*

PHILIP. How's that for a miracle?

ALAN. That wasn't a miracle.

PHILIP. If you think getting Miss Jones up here in her negligee isn't a miracle – you don't know Miss Jones.

ALAN. You'd better stay away from her.

PHILIP. Why?

ALAN. If Rigsby finds out –

PHILIP. He won't. Do you know why? He doesn't want to find out – his pride wouldn't stand it.

ALAN. I wouldn't be too sure about that. He says she's a dam ready to burst – and when it does – he'll be waiting.

PHILIP. How does he know the dam hasn't burst already?

ALAN. You're playing with fire.

PHILIP. *(shrugs)* I've tried to discourage her.

ALAN. You weren't discouraging her tonight.

PHILIP. You were here. What could have happened?

(He helps **ALAN** *with the bed.)*

In fact, you could do me a favour.

ALAN. What favour?

PHILIP. By never leaving me alone with her.

ALAN. Why?

PHILIP. I'm moving on. I've met someone else.

ALAN. Oh.

PHILIP. But I don't want to hurt her feelings. It would be kinder to do it this way.

ALAN. Why are you tired of her?

PHILIP. *(studies him)* That surprises you, doesn't it? You like her.

ALAN. I haven't thought about it. I've only just met her.

PHILIP. I could see she liked you. You're the sort of person she likes.

ALAN. I thought you were the sort of person she likes.

PHILIP. I think she'd prefer someone more...unspoilt – someone she could mould. She's a great moulder.

ALAN. Well, she's not moulding me. Not with Rigsby up and down the stairs. I'm not ending up behind the wallpaper.

PHILIP. You'd be surprised how attractive she is...

ALAN. Would I?

PHILIP. She has a beautiful back...

ALAN. Has she?

PHILIP. Goes on for miles.

ALAN. I'm not interested.

PHILIP. Who is it your afraid of, Alan? Rigsby or Ruth?

ALAN. Rigsby.

PHILIP. Are you a virgin?

ALAN. Certainly not!

PHILIP. But it is your first time away from home?

ALAN. *(blustering)* Yes but that has nothing to do with it. Why do you think I left home? I had to get out of that place. Her parents came round. There was quite a scene. They said it was my fault she failed her A-Levels.

PHILIP. She was still at school?

ALAN. Only just. Last year. Out of uniform. Very mature.

PHILIP. Ruth's very mature.

ALAN. If she's so wonderful why are you moving on?

PHILIP. We're not compatible. She will dramatise the situation. She will put her hand on mine and say with a sigh, "Black on white, Philip." It makes me cringe. I feel I'm just another good cause – like famine relief. That it's all some sort of tragedy with her as the heroine.

ALAN. Well, I'm not going with a drama queen. If you don't mind I'll make my own friends –

(ALAN breaks off as RUTH backs abruptly into the room.)

PHILIP. Ruth! What's the matter?

RUTH. He's outside my door. I know he is. I've been standing on the stairs hardly daring to breathe.

PHILIP. Are you sure?

(PHILIP wedges a chair against the door.)

RUTH. I saw the glow of his cigarette. He always forgets – it always gives him away. If he finds me here…

ALAN. What can he do?

RUTH. He cuts my water off.

PHILIP. He's coming up the stairs.

RUTH. What should I do?

(PHILIP sighs and opens the wardrobe door. RUTH steps inside. PHILIP closes the door. The outer door rattles. PHILIP removes the chair. RIGSBY enters. He looks around suspiciously.)

PHILIP. When are we going to get a key for that door, Rigsby?

RIGSBY. Why? Got something to hide?

PHILIP. There's such a thing as privacy.

RIGSBY. We don't need keys here. At least we didn't. Besides, I have to have access…

(He looks around.)

PHILIP. Well? What did you want?

RIGSBY. I thought I heard a crash...

(He crosses to bedroom moving **ALAN** *out of the way. He stares in horror at the wreckage of the bed. He looks indignantly at* **ALAN.***)* What's happened here?

ALAN. The bed collapsed.

RIGSBY. I can see that. I want to know why.

ALAN. It wasn't put up properly.

RIGSBY. Of course it was put up properly. There's been horseplay.

ALAN. No.

RIGSBY. You've only been here five minutes and look at the place. This is vandalism. I'll need a deposit from you against damages. That bed would have taken any normal wear. What have you been up to?

ALAN. Nothing.

RIGSBY. I've been wrong about you. I thought you'd be a civilising influence.

PHILIP. What do you mean – civilising?

RIGSBY. I can do without all this upheaval. Crashing and banging in the middle of the night. I need peace and quiet. I had a bad war. You only have to burst a paper bag behind me and I'd be over that settee. I don't need riotous students.

(He crosses to the windows.)

And draw these curtains.

(He draws them savagely.)

PHILIP. Why? Who can see in?

RIGSBY. That's not the point. This house is a landmark – it's like a beacon – and we're on a bombing run.

*(***PHILIP** *and* **ALAN** *look at each other and laugh.)*

ALAN. A bombing run!

RIGSBY. You can laugh. But this is the way they'll come. Straight from the Urals. Nothing to stop them. Pre-emptive strike.

ALAN. You don't believe that, surely?

RIGSBY. Why not?

ALAN. It's mad.

RIGSBY. It's a mad situation. I'm not saying it's rational. But do you think Brezhnev's rational?

ALAN. Isn't he?

RIGSBY. He's got a time-lock on his cigarette case. That doesn't say much for self-control, does it? One of these days he'll feel like a fag – find he can't get into his case until five – bingo – World War 3. And this place will be a nuclear swamp.

PHILIP. In that case I don't know why you're making so much fuss about the bed. And I need some sleep.

ALAN. So do I.

RIGSBY. You're not interested, are you? Well, just remember – it won't be me who has to go next time – it'll be you.

ALAN. I'm not going. I'd sooner be red than dead.

RIGSBY. *(explodes)* I knew it! I knew there was something odd about you. You're a pacifist.

ALAN. I'm going to be a doctor. I happen to believe that life is sacred.

RIGSBY. You mean yours is. You're like the last bloke – he was a medical student. He thought his life was sacred. Always taking his temperature – blood pressure – analysing his water. Very strange he was.

(RIGSBY crosses to the carpet and straightens it with his foot.)

He thought his shoulder blades were deformed. I assured him they weren't but he wouldn't listen. Always trying to see them in the mirror. By the time he'd finished they were deformed.

PHILIP. We would like to get some sleep, Rigsby.

(RIGSBY looks up from the carpet. His glance seizes on ALAN.)

RIGSBY. Has she been up?

ALAN. Who?

RIGSBY. Miss Jones?

ALAN. No.

RIGSBY. Now that surprises me. I thought she'd have been up to welcome you. She takes a great interest in her students...

ALAN. *(hesitates)* She did come up earlier.

RIGSBY. You said she hadn't.

ALAN. I thought you meant recently.

RIGSBY. Nice, isn't she?

ALAN. Yes.

RIGSBY. She's certainly raised the tone around here.

ALAN. Has she?

RIGSBY. A woman of refinement. She's responsible for the blue water in the toilet. And the shades over the bulbs on the landing. Things you don't think about. It's called good taste. You should see her table mats – scenes from the ballet. How many people eat off scenes from the ballet? Unfortunately, although she has good taste she's a poor judge of character. It's her only flaw. She believes in people. But I don't. That's why I keep an eye out for her – in case someone tries to take advantage...

ALAN. Do they do that?

RIGSBY. Sometimes...I'll say goodnight then.

ALAN. Goodnight.

(RIGSBY crosses to the door.)

PHILIP. Goodnight, Rigsby.

RIGSBY. Goodnight.

(He opens the wardrobe door. Reproachfully.)

Goodnight, Miss Jones.

RUTH. *(quietly)* Mr Rigsby...

    (**RIGSBY** *exits.*)

    (Lights fade.)

    (Curtain.)

Scene Three

(The attic flat. Next morning.)

(PHILIP is alone. He is finishing a piece of toast and dressing to go out. RIGSBY enters. He looks narrowly around the room.)

RIGSBY. Where is he?

PHILIP. Who?

RIGSBY. Your friend.

PHILIP. He's not my friend. I thought he was your friend.

RIGSBY. Well, he's not. Where is he?

PHILIP. Gone for a paper.

RIGSBY. I didn't hear him go. I think he's avoiding me. *(pause)* Have you noticed something about him? He never meets your eye.

PHILIP. He's probably shy.

RIGSBY. He's not shy. You can't say he's shy after last night. And he's not the only one who's avoiding me. There's Miss Jones.

PHILIP. What makes you think she's avoiding you?

RIGSBY. *(stares)* What makes me think it? When I walk into a room and someone steps into the wardrobe I naturally assume that person's avoiding me.

PHILIP. She was embarrassed.

RIGSBY. She was also in her nightdress.

PHILIP. That's why she was embarrassed – and confused. She knows you have a high opinion of her. She didn't want to lose it.

RIGSBY. Did she say that?

PHILIP. After you'd gone. Apparently it means a great deal to her.

RIGSBY. Oh. *(pause)* Why was she in her nightdress?

PHILIP. She was going to bed.

RIGSBY. I know that! But what was she doing up here?

PHILIP. She heard the crash and came to investigate. Perfectly natural.

RIGSBY. Then why didn't he say? Was he embarrassed as well?

PHILIP. Of course.

RIGSBY. I don't think he's as innocent as he looks. He's a Methodist and they're sex mad.

PHILIP. *(smiles)* I didn't know that.

RIGSBY. Well known for it. *(pause)* He said he didn't know her but it could be all very convenient – getting him in here.

PHILIP. She didn't get him in here. *(pause)* She got me in here.

RIGSBY. What?

PHILIP. You could say the same about me.

RIGSBY. *(hesitates)* Ah but you're different.

PHILIP. Am I?

(RIGSBY *eyes him curiously.*)

RIGSBY. He says you've got ten wives.

PHILIP. Yes, well, I think it's ten.

RIGSBY. God! Ten wives!

PHILIP. Why not? I'm not poor. I'm not sick.

RIGSBY. *(bitterly)* One was enough for me.

PHILIP. It didn't work out?

RIGSBY. It was a disaster on the scale of Anzio. I married in haste – you did in those days. There was a troopship leaving and you snatched at happiness. You didn't expect much – you didn't get much. We were on ration then. *(broodingly)* I've been on bloody ration ever since. *(pause)* He says you're the son of a chief.

PHILIP. Yes.

RIGSBY. Do you have power over women?

PHILIP. Yes.

RIGSBY. *(grins)* Yes. You make them walk miles in the sun with pots on their heads, don't you?

PHILIP. They don't seem to mind.

RIGSBY. Ours would. They'd say they'd got a headache. Ours are always getting headaches. Do yours get headaches?

PHILIP. No but they lead a more natural life.

RIGSBY. Yes, you're closer to nature. I haven't been close to nature since last Christmas. *(pause)* I wasn't that close then.

(He studies **PHILIP.** *)*

Son of a chief. I suppose you come from an old family?

PHILIP. From the beginning of time.

RIGSBY. They always made the best officers. They were born to it. Not like those who came up through the ranks. They hadn't the authority. You have to be born to command. Like my old captain – he came from a good family. Always carried a walking stick and smoked a pipe. Never wore a tin hat. Never saw him ruffled. When Jerry opened up he'd just lean on his stick and say, "where do you think that's coming from, sergeant?" Everyone would dive for cover but not the captain.

PHILIP. What happened to him?

RIGSBY. *(frowns)* He got blown up by a shell.

*(***PHILIP*** suppresses a smile.)*

PHILIP. Well, I've got a lecture.

(He makes for the door. **RIGSBY** *catches his arm.)*

RIGSBY. She said that, did she?

PHILIP. What?

RIGSBY. That she valued my good opinion.

PHILIP. Yes.

RIGSBY. So you don't think I'm wasting my time?

PHILIP. No.

RIGSBY. But I don't seem to be getting anywhere and I'm running out of time. I can't get her into conversation. I thought she might be interested in my war experiences but she never wants to listen.

PHILIP. That surprises me. It worked with Desdemona.

RIGSBY. *(uncertainly)* Did it?

PHILIP. Othello did it all the time.

RIGSBY. Othello?

PHILIP. "When I spake of most disastrous chances, of battles, sieges, fortunes, that I have passed – of moving accident by flood and field – of hairbreadth scapes in the imminent deadly breach..."

RIGSBY. Well, I've had my share of those.

PHILIP. "To this Desdemona would seriously incline and with a greedy ear devour my discourse."

RIGSBY. Well, it may have worked for Othello – I usually end up talking to myself. *(sighs)* I sometimes wonder if it's worth it.

PHILIP. Rigsby, we have a flower in my country – it blooms every ten years and you have to climb the highest peak to see it. But when you do see it...

RIGSBY. Yes?

PHILIP. It's wonderful. Breathtaking. It's certainly worth it.

*(***RIGSBY** *follows him to the door.)*

RIGSBY. And you say it worked for this...?

PHILIP. Othello? Yes. But he did have one great advantage over you.

RIGSBY. What was that?

PHILIP. He was black.

*(***PHILIP** *exits.* **RIGSBY** *stares after him, slightly puzzled. He turns his attention to the room. He checks that the bed has been properly erected. He pulls back the carpet and studies the floor.)*

*(***ALAN** *enters cautiously. He freezes when he sees* **RIGSBY**. **RIGSBY** *sees him.)*

RIGSBY. This hole's getting bigger.

ALAN. Is it?

(He snatches his books from the bedroom. **RIGSBY** *cuts him off at the door.)*

RIGSBY. Where do you think you're going?

ALAN. I've got a lecture.

RIGSBY. I want a word with you.

ALAN. What about?

RIGSBY. What was she doing in the wardrobe?

ALAN. Hiding.

RIGSBY. I know that! I want to know why?

ALAN. Don't ask me. I was asleep.

RIGSBY. You weren't asleep when I came in. And what about the bed? Explain that. I'm very disappointed in you. I was taken in by the bible.

ALAN. My mother packed it.

RIGSBY. She probably thought you'd need it. Your behaviour has been very un-Christian. Thou shalt not lie. That's one of the Ten Commandments.

ALAN. No it isn't.

RIGSBY. Isn't it?

ALAN. No.

RIGSBY. Then it should be. And why was she in a negligee? All the time she's been here I've never seen her in a negligee. You get a butcher's on your first night.

(He crosses to the window.)

I've only seen her underwear dancing on that washing line. She still wears harvest festivals – all is safely gathered in. That's the sort of woman she is – modest, refined. And suddenly it's a negligee. Nothing prepared me for that. It was as if it was a special occasion. Was it a special occasion?

ALAN. Why ask me? I'm not the only one who lives here.

RIGSBY. You're the one who concerns me at the moment.

ALAN. I'm sure it was all perfectly innocent.

RIGSBY. Then why did her ears go red?

ALAN. Did they?

RIGSBY. Bright red. I've never seen them that colour before. There was guilt written all over her. A woman who eats off scenes from the ballet reduced to cowering in a wardrobe with crimson ears. Well, I've marked your card. I'm watching you.

(He takes hold of ALAN*'s collar.)*

You're lucky the magistrate won't allow me one more punch...

*(*RUTH *enters. She is wearing short skirt, knee length socks, medallions and bangles.* RIGSBY *gently releases* ALAN *and pretends to be adjusting his collar.)*

RUTH. I was just going to the shops – can I – *(she breaks off)* Mr Rigsby.

RIGSBY. Miss Jones.

(He scowls from one to the other and exits.)

RUTH. Alan, what ever you do – never leave me alone with that man.

(She makes sure the door is closed.)

ALAN. *(wearily)* Oh, no.

RUTH. What's the matter?

ALAN. I think we're going to se a lot of each other.

RUTH. What do you mean?

ALAN. *(hesitates)* I mean...Rigsby's one ambition is to get close to you.

RUTH. I know. He gives me the creeps. He's a very creepy person. I feel he's always watching me. Even when I'm alone in my room I feel these eyes boring into me.

*(*ALAN *glances uneasily at the carpet.)*

ALAN. That must be awful.

RUTH. It is.

ALAN. Did he cut your water off?

RUTH. It was the merest trickle this morning.

ALAN. Why don't you leave?

RUTH. I was going to.

(The bangles on her arms become agitated and she constantly pushes them back.)

And then Philip came – and everything changed. He needs me.

ALAN. *(doubtfully)* Does he?

RUTH. And accommodation is so difficult.

ALAN. I know – I wouldn't be here if it wasn't.

RUTH. Alan, you won't say anything to Rigsby? We have to be discreet.

ALAN. Philip wasn't very discreet last night. Why does he do that?

RUTH. He loves to embarrass me. He likes to see me blush. They can't do that, you see.

ALAN. You mean the ten wives?

RUTH. He mentioned those, did he?

ALAN. Yes.

RUTH. He says my blushes remind him of the sun rising over the Serengeti. He can say wonderful poetic things. Terribly deep. Things that make you think. He says I'm a pool without water yet men may drown in me. That's very poetic, isn't it?

ALAN. Yes. What does it mean?

RUTH. *(hesitates)* I'm not sure. But it is incredibly deep.

ALAN. *(smiles)* Deeper than the pool.

(RUTH stares. He realises she has no sense of humour.)

RUTH. He says I have the skin of fruit and beautiful milk. That's very basic, isn't it?

ALAN. Yes – I think the bit about the milk's very basic.

RUTH. You know, I like you, Alan. I think we're going to be friends.

ALAN. I hope so.

RUTH. They say three's a crowd but it could be an advantage.

ALAN. Could it?

RUTH. I could be coming to see you.

ALAN. No – I don't think that's a good idea.

RUTH. Why not? It would put Rigsby off our track.

ALAN. But it would put him on my track, Ruth.

RUTH. *(amused)* You and me? No one would possibly think that, Alan.

ALAN. *(disappointed)* Wouldn't they?

RUTH. You could slip out when we wanted to be alone.

ALAN. Slip out?

RUTH. To the pictures – or somewhere.

ALAN. Ruth – I have to work. Couldn't Philip come down to you?

RUTH. No. Rigsby's always hanging around my door. He's painted it three times this month. It's not as if he'd understand. He's so bigoted. He reminds me of my father. My father wanted to keep Britain white. He'd get so choleric on the subject I told him he'd have a heart attack. And he did.

ALAN. Your father's dead?

RUTH. He died on Guy Fawkes night on the way to post an angry letter to the *Times* on the subject. He collapsed in the street. People kept stepping over him – they thought he was a guy.

ALAN. That must have been terrible.

RUTH. It was. There was four and six in his cap when they found him. Not much for a man's life, Alan.

*(She chokes back a sob. **ALAN** puts an arm around her shoulder.)*

Thank you, Alan.

ALAN. Ruth, is there a Mrs Rigsby?

RUTH. There was once – when I first came here. Then one night when I arrived home I heard shouts and footsteps on the stairs. Rigsby came dashing by me, blood gushing from him – his wife was running after him. I wasn't sure whether it was to administer succour or the *coup-de-grâce.* Sometimes I'm so frightened...

(ALAN holds her close.)

ALAN. You mustn't be. I'm here now.

RUTH. You don't know what it feels like being watched all the time...

(RIGSBY enters abruptly. **RUTH** *and* **ALAN** *spring apart. Rigsby regards them even more suspiciously. He is holding something behind his back.)*

(RUTH gives him a curt nod and exits.)

RIGSBY. That does it. I hoped it wouldn't come to this – but it has.

ALAN. Come to what?

RIGSBY: A fight.

(He takes two pairs of boxing gloves and lays them on the table.)

Take your choice....

(ALAN backs away nervously.)

ALAN. What are those for?

RIGSBY. Well, they're not to stop you biting your nails or any other unseemly nocturnal activity. These are for the fight.

ALAN. What about the magistrates?

RIGSBY. I'm not talking about a brawl. I'm talking about a sporting contest.

ALAN. How sporting?

RIGSBY. Queensberry Rules. Take your pick.

(He pushes the gloves towards him.)

ALAN. (*peers closer*) What are those marks?

RIGSBY. Well, it's not tomato sauce...

ALAN. You mean it's...

RIGSBY. Dried blood – not mine I hasten to add.

(ALAN *retreats.*)

ALAN. I'm not putting those on!

RIGSBY. Don't look like that. I'm not going to hurt you.

ALAN. (*hopefully*) You're not?

RIGSBY. You won't feel a thing. Everything will go dark, that's all.

ALAN. I'm not waiting for everything to go dark!

(*He tries to move away but* RIGSBY *restrains him.*)

RIGSBY. Look on the bright side.

ALAN. What bright side?

RIGSBY. You could win. You've got youth on your side.

(RIGSBY *holds onto him.*)

And there's a prize....

ALAN. What's that?

RIGSBY. Miss Jones.

ALAN. Miss Jones? I'm not interested.

RIGSBY. Oh, yes you are. It's too late to back out now. I tried to warn you off but you wouldn't listen. You've started enticing her up here.

ALAN. I haven't.

RIGSBY. She's practically living up here. Now give me a hand with this table...

ALAN. Why?

RIGSBY. We need more space – if someone's going to go crashing to the ground..

ALAN. Crashing to the ground? You mean me, don't you?

RIGSBY. Don't be defeatist. It could be either one of us.

ALAN. It couldn't – because I'm not fighting.

RIGSBY. You've no choice. If you win I'll step back. Doesn't that tempt you?

ALAN. No.

RIGSBY. It does me. That's why I need to prove I'm the better man.

ALAN. I'll tell her!

RIGSBY. That won't do it. She won't believe that until she sees you stretched out like a roll of lino.

ALAN. You're not stretching me out like a roll of lino.

(PHILIP *enters.*)

(ALAN *ducks behind him.*)

Keep him off me!

PHILIP. (*sternly*) That's enough Rigsby.

RIGSBY. Out of my way – unless you want a taste of the same.

PHILIP. (*smiles*) I don't mind.

RIGSBY. (*stares*) What?

PHILIP. But I'll change my shirt first. Don't want to get blood on it...

(*He gives* RIGSBY *a friendly pat and exits.* RIGSBY *looks after him a shade uneasily.*)

RIGSBY. I thought he looked worried, didn't you?

ALAN. No.

RIGSBY. Definitely turned pale.

ALAN. I didn't notice.

RIGSBY. Well, it's hard to tell...

(RIGSBY *continues swinging punches.*)

ALAN. You know when he said he didn't want to get blood on his shirt...

RIGSBY. Yeh?

ALAN. Do you think he meant yours?

RIGSBY. He won't lay a glove on me.

ALAN. He's never lost yet...

RIGSBY. He's never met me.

ALAN. He was a champion in his country.

RIGSBY. (*anxiously*) Was he? Well, they wouldn't dare knock
him down – he's the son of a chief. If they tried that
they'd find themselves skinned alive and stretched
over a set of drums. I'll tie him in knots, don't you
worry.

ALAN. Suppose he ties you in knots?

RIGSBY. I'll work him over inside.

ALAN. Suppose he works *you* over inside?

RIGSBY. I'll give him my rapier-like left and my vicious right
hook.

ALAN. Suppose he gives you his rapier-like left and his
vicious right hook?

RIGSBY. (*angrily*) Will you stop supposing! (*Pause*) Then I'll
talk him out of it. That's what his mate Ali does. Talks
them to death. He gets them in a clinch – engages in
a bit of witty repartee and while they're trying to think
of an answer he clouts them round the ear.

ALAN. Is that what you're going to do?

RIGSBY. Psychology, I'll put the frighteners on him. You
know what they say, 'If you can't fight – wear a big
hat...'

(ALAN *begins to move the furniture. He checks the
amount of space.* RIGSBY *watches uneasily.*)

What are you doing?

ALAN. Making sure there's room for you to fall.

(RIGSBY *continues to look more anxious.*)

RIGSBY. That reminds me. Miss Jones is just below here.
She'll hear what's going on. Better tell her.

ALAN. Tell her what?

RIGSBY. That men are fighting over her. (*Slyly*) Of course,
she may not approve... She's against acts of violence. I
mean she's trying to ban Polaris. She ought to be told.

ALAN. But she'll stop it.

RIGSBY. She may. It'll be a disappointment but we have to
respect her wishes. Off you go.

(ALAN *exits reluctantly.* RIGSBY *returns to throwing punches.*)

(PHILIP *enters. He is stripped to shorts and vest. He watches* RIGSBY *impassively. He slips on gloves. He moves into a corner and throws a few punches. They watch each other.*)

PHILIP. Ready?

RIGSBY. Waiting for Alan.

PHILIP. Why?

RIGSBY. Referee.

PHILIP. Do we need one?

RIGSBY. Oh, yes. I only fight under Queensberry Rules.

PHILIP. You seem to have had a lot of experience.

RIGSBY. Regimental Champion.

PHILIP. You don't look like one.

RIGSBY. You mean because I'm unmarked? Don't let these classic good looks fool you. We are the ones you have to look out for. They could never lay a glove on me. And do you know why? Reflexes.

PHILIP. (*doubtfully*) Reflexes?

RIGSBY. I've always been able to ride a punch. I float like a butterfly and sting like a bee. Come on, punch me.

PHILIP. Punch you?

RIGSBY. I haven't lost it. I may look old in years but inside I'm like a coiled spring.

(RIGSBY *sticks out his chin.*)

Come on, your best shot.

PHILIP. I don't like to.

RIGSBY. You won't hurt me. And don't telegraph it. Try and take me by surprise – not that you –

(PHILIP *throws a sudden straight left.* RIGSBY *spins round, almost falls and then begins to weave around in a daze. He appears to be searching for his opponent.*)

PHILIP. (*politely*) Over here, Rigsby.

(RIGSBY *staggers over to* PHILIP. *He aims a punch and finishes being suipported by* PHILIP.)

(ALAN *bursts in.*)

ALAN. Ruth says it's all right – in fact she's flattered. (*He breaks off*) What's he doing?

PHILIP. He's floating like a butterfly. What was that about Ruth?

ALAN. She says she'll go out with the winner – the last man standing. She knows it'll be you...

(PHILIP *looks horrified.*)

PHILIP. Oh, no...

(*He allows himself to sink to the floor with the now comatose* RIGSBY.)

ALAN. What are you doing?

PHILIP. You take her. You're the last man standing...

(*The door opens suddenly.* RUTH *enters dressed to kill.*)

RUTH. To the victor the spoils....

(ALAN *sinks to the floor. She surveys the three recumbent forms.*)

Oh...

(*Curtain.*)

ACT TWO

(The attic flat. A year later. Evening. ALAN *and* PHILIP *are preparing to go out. The year has seen a marked change in* ALAN. *He has lost his conservative, buttoned-up look. His casual clothes are in fashion. His hair is no longer neatly combed. He is wearing an earring. Only a slightly nervous manner recalls the year before.)*

ALAN. What time did you say we'd be there?

PHILIP. About nine.

ALAN. What's mine like?

PHILIP. Sweet, sensitive – nice nature.

*(*ALAN *considers this.)*

ALAN. You mean she's ugly?

PHILIP. No. She's very attractive.

ALAN. Good. *(pause)* Then why am I getting her?

PHILIP. She's a friend of this girl. They insisted on a foursome. I promised to find someone presentable.

ALAN. *(pleased)* And you thought of me.

PHILIP. No, he couldn't get – then I thought of you.

*(*ALAN *throws a cushion at him.* ALAN *crosses to the mirror.)*

ALAN. Suppose Ruth finds out?

PHILIP. She won't – unless you tell her.

ALAN. I won't tell her. We're friends, aren't we? *(pause)* Do you think I look all right? Or do you think I should change?

PHILIP. You've changed twice already. Try and relax.

ALAN. I am relaxed. What do you think of the earring? Do you think they'll go for it?

(**PHILIP** *studies the earring.*)

PHILIP. Yes, I like it. It looks as if you don't give a damn.

ALAN. I don't.

PHILIP. Has Rigsby seen it yet?

ALAN. No. I've been covering it with my hand. I know what he'll say. He'll say it's effeminate. *(pause)* You did say about nine?

PHILIP. Yes. Don't worry – I've ordered a taxi.

ALAN. *(impressed)* A taxi. Hey. Do you think we should take these?

(*He picks up a pill box from the shelf.*)

PHILIP. What are they?

ALAN. Pills. I got them from a bloke in the last year. He's getting married – doesn't need them anymore.

PHILIP. What do they do?

ALAN. They're relaxants – they make you sleepy but responsive...

PHILIP. *(stares)* You're not suggesting we drug them?

ALAN. No.

(**PHILIP** *returns the tablets to shelf.*)

PHILIP. How did your friend get them?

ALAN. They were taken off the wards.

PHILIP. Why?

ALAN. They have these side effects.

PHILIP. What side effects?

ALAN. They turn your water green.

PHILIP. Green?

ALAN. Bright green.

PHILIP. Well, we can certainly do without that.

(*He picks up a towel.*)

ALAN. Where are you going?

PHILIP. For a wash.

ALAN. There won't be time! We'll be late. Why couldn't you have done that earlier?

PHILIP. There's plenty of time. Calm down. Read a book.

(He throws a copy of "Playboy" at ALAN and exits. ALAN puts book down and crosses to mirror and checks his earring. He crosses to the skeleton.)

ALAN. Hello, darling. I must say you look ravishing tonight. And what a captivating smile. Would you care for the next dance?

(ALAN begins to whirl the skeleton around the room.)

You dance divinely – you're as light as a feather. Have you lost weight? Oh – Weightwatchers? Well, they seem to have done the trick. It's just dropped off you.

(RIGSBY enters. ALAN whirls around to be confronted by him)

RIGSBY. You morbid sod.

ALAN. Where's your sense of humour, Rigsby?

(He sings 'them bones, them bones, them dry bones.')

RIGSBY. *(stares)* What's that?

ALAN. *(uneasily)* What?

RIGSBY. What's that – glinting in your ear?

ALAN. An earring.

RIGSBY. An earring! My God! Why should England tremble?

ALAN. What's wrong with it?

RIGSBY. It's effeminate – that's what's wrong with it. I'm getting worried about you – it's all that white wine you've been drinking. This wouldn't have happened if you'd stuck to pints.

ALAN. Everyone's wearing them these days.

RIGSBY. Then God help this country. I just hope the Russians don't find out. I can just see us all marching into battle in earrings. That should send a thrill of fear through the enemy. *(studies the earring)* Suppose you catch it in something?

ALAN. *(stares)* Catch it in what?

RIGSBY. I had a friend – caught his signet ring in the door handle of a taxi – tore his finger off.

ALAN. Rigsby, I don't close doors with my ear.

RIGSBY. All right. But if you come back with an ear missing – don't blame me.

(ALAN returns to the mirror. RIGSBY eyes him enviously.)

RIGSBY. Going out?

ALAN. Yes.

RIGSBY. I wondered why you were preening yourself.

ALAN. I'm not preening myself.

RIGSBY. You were in the bathroom for hours. It's swimming in water.

ALAN. I was washing my hair.

RIGSBY. And that's getting too long. You came out of that bathroom looking like Veronica Lake.

ALAN. Who's Veronica Lake?

RIGSBY. *(sighs)* She was a film star – well known for her long, flowing hair. You're a lot like her – except she wore less jewellery.

ALAN. Look, I'm taking a little more trouble with my appearance because I'm going on a date.

RIGSBY. *(enviously)* A date?

ALAN. Yes.

RIGSBY. Well, you've certainly changed since you came here with your ivory prayer book.

(He picks up a magazine.)

Now it's *Playboy*. It's disgusting.

ALAN. There's nothing disgusting about the female form. Evil is in the eye of the beholder.

RIGSBY. But I'm not doing the beholding, am I? I don't spend all day looking at the centrefold. It'll come as a great surprise to you when you find they haven't got staples across their navels.

ALAN. Don't you worry – I've seen a few navels in my time. Oh, and don't wait up tonight – I'll be late, very late.

(RIGSBY continues to watch him enviously.)

RIGSBY. It's going to be like that, is it?

ALAN. Just let's say there'll be another notch on the bedpost by morning.

RIGSBY. You mean you keep a score? You know what you'd have been in the war – a bloody sniper.

ALAN. Eat your heart out, Rigsby. Tonight I shall be visiting the erogenous zones...

RIGSBY. *(stares)* The erogenous zones?

ALAN. *(smiles)* You don't know what they are, do you?

RIGSBY. Of course.

ALAN. Where are they?

RIGSBY. Somewhere near the equator, aren't they?

ALAN. The erogenous zones are parts of the body most sensitive to sexual stimuli.

RIGSBY. Oh, those erogenous zones.

ALAN. You don't know where they are, do you?

(RIGSBY considers this and finally breaks the silence.)

RIGSBY. *(hesitates)* Refresh my memory.

ALAN. Well, there's the inside of the leg.

RIGSBY. I know that! But I can't start there. What would she say?

ALAN. Are you talking about Miss Jones?

RIGSBY. I'm not saying who I'm talking about. Can't we move a bit further up?

ALAN. There are the breasts...

RIGSBY. You're doing it again! I know about the breasts. I couldn't put my hand there. I can just see her face. "What do you think you're doing," she'd say. She's a respectable woman.

ALAN. No woman's respectable where the erogenous zones are concerned.

RIGSBY. That's what you think. In my day you'd get your face slapped. Things were different then. The purity of a woman was important. It was the finest gift she could give her husband on their wedding night. Now he has to make do with a set of cufflinks.

ALAN. Times have changed, Rigsby.

RIGSBY. They certainly have. I was married before I was your age. That was during the war. We were married with gas mask cases over our shoulders. I could see prospects were bleak from the outset. Two tiers of the wedding cake were cardboard – that was an omen. Everything was second hand – even the confetti was covered in heel marks. It was called a period of austerity. I don't think I've ever come out of it. And I'm not getting any younger. I sometimes look at my old army photos. All the blokes standing there with their arms folded – all grinning away. Some have crosses over them – the ones that bought it – but they're grinning just as much as the others. You see you never know when time's running out...

ALAN. *(sympathetically)* And you haven't replaced yourself.

RIGSBY. No.

ALAN. Never mind. A man can do that in his eighties.

RIGSBY. *(explodes)* I'm not waiting that long!

ALAN. You could blow in her ear.

RIGSBY. What?

ALAN. That's an erogenous zone.

RIGSBY. Is it?

ALAN. You'd be surprised at the results...

RIGSBY. Results?

ALAN. Sea breaking against the rocks – rockets launching into space – trains hurtling through tunnels. And in the background, Rachmaninov...

RIGSBY. *(dryly)* What's he doing there?

ALAN. Not him – his music.

RIGSBY. I know what you mean but I don't get close enough to blow in her ear. She's never still – always so agitated. Normally I'm a good conversationalist – you must have noticed that – but not with her. I'm too tense – I can't relax.

(ALAN passes him the pill box.)

ALAN. Then take a couple of these.

RIGSBY. What are they?

ALAN. Tranquillisers.

RIGSBY. Tranquillisers?

ALAN. They'll relax you – and at the same time arouse you...

RIGSBY. I don't need pills for that.

(He studies the box suspiciously.)

They haven't got hormones in them, have they?

ALAN. No. Why?

RIGSBY. They can have a very strange effect. I don't want my voice breaking while I'm talking to her.

ALAN. You'll be all right, but don't take more than a couple – they're quite strong. And there's some white wine in the fridge – it's yours if you want it. She's very partial to white wine.

RIGSBY. Is she?

ALAN. Yes. And try some French phrases – that usually helps.

RIGSBY. French?

ALAN. Yes. A few French phrases in the ear – that can be very stimulating.

RIGSBY. I didn't know that.

ALAN. Do you know any French?

RIGSBY. Of course I do. *(pause)* You seem to know a lot about this.

ALAN. Don't let my youthful looks fool you, Rigsby. I've been around.

RIGSBY. I bet you have, you young rip.

(They're grinning at each other when PHILIP *enters. He looks from one to the other. He begins to slip on his jacket.)*

PHILIP. See if the taxi's come, Alan.

ALAN. The taxi – of course.

*(*ALAN *dashes from the room.)*

PHILIP. What was all that about?

RIGSBY. He was giving me some advice on my love life. Giving me the benefit of his experience.

PHILIP. Well, that shouldn't have taken long – you haven't got any love life and he hasn't had any experience.

RIGSBY. I don't know about that. You'd be surprised at the things he comes out with. Although you're right about my love life. It's non-existent. I don't get many chances these days. There was this woman in the pub. They all said, don't give her a lift home or she'll interfere with you while you were driving. *(pause)* So I gave her a lift home.

PHILIP. *(grins)* What happened?

RIGSBY. *(bitterly)* Nothing. She was a washout. Talked about her feet all the time.

PHILIP. Well, at least you've saved yourself for Miss Jones.

RIGSBY. Yes, but a man can only save himself for so long. I'm running out of time and patience. What would you do? You've got ten wives – you must know something.

PHILIP. Well, in my country, if a man were in your position he'd take the wood from the love tree and burn it outside the girl's hut. She would smell the smoke – appear at the door – look into the man's eyes and fall deeply in love with him.

*(*RIGSBY *stares in awed silence.)*

RIGSBY. Just like that?

PHILIP. It never fails.

RIGSBY. Because they believe it, I suppose.

PHILIP. I suppose so. But of course we are a primitive people.

RIGSBY. Yes. *(pause)* Got any of this wood?

PHILIP. I did bring some over...

RIGSBY. I wouldn't mind seeing it...

PHILIP. But you don't believe it?

RIGSBY. I'm sure it works for them. But you're dealing with a sophisticated European here. But I wouldn't mind seeing it...

*(**PHILIP** crosses to the wardrobe and returns with a piece of wood. Hands it to **RIGSBY**.)*

RIGSBY. Thanks. Very interesting.

*(He examines the wood. **PHILIP** makes for the door.)*

Hey. This has been planed.

PHILIP. *(shrugs)* Everything's commercial these days, Rigsby.

*(**PHILIP** exits. **RIGSBY** puts the wood down and looks thoughtfully around the room. He crosses to the fridge and takes out bottle of wine. He places it on coffee table along with two glasses. Studies the effect. Sound of car departing. He crosses to bedroom and looks out. He picks up a bottle of aftershave. Reads the label.)*

RIGSBY. "A blend of oriental herbs and spices – from a secret recipe known only to the eunuchs." Hm.

(He douses himself with it. Studies himself in the mirror. Undoes a button on his shirt. He takes a medallion from the dresser and slips it on. He slicks down his hair. He takes a deep breath. He takes the discarded love wood and taps three times on the floor.)

(He pours the wine. He swallows two of the tablets. Hesitates and takes two more. He picks up a record and looks at the label.)

Rachmaninov – that should do it.

(He places record on turntable. He hears a sound on the stairs and waits. RUTH *makes an eager entrance and sees* RIGSBY...*she hesitates and looks round.)*

RUTH. Mr Rigsby. I thought the boys were here...

RIGSBY. They'll be back in a minute, Miss Jones. They said, would you wait.

RUTH. *(uncertainly)* Did they?

RIGSBY. They made a point of it. Ask her to wait, they said. Even left you a glass of wine...

(He crosses and motions to the wine.)

You are partial to white wine, Miss Jones?

RUTH. Well, yes – but I could always come back...

RIGSBY. No, they were insistent. Ask her to wait – entertain her, they said.

RUTH. Entertain me?

RIGSBY. *(suavely)* Why don't you dispose of yourself on the settee, Miss Jones?

*(*RUTH *sits reluctantly. She observes the second glass nervously.* RIGSBY *sits by her and raises his glass.)*

Down the hatch.

*(*RUTH *sips her wine and looks around.)*

RUTH. Where have they gone?

RIGSBY. Who?

RUTH. Alan and Philip.

RIGSBY. I don't know. But if you don't mind me saying – you worry too much about those two. Students. You can't depend on them. I know the seed packet promises a riot of colour but what do you get? Cabbages.

RUTH. Cabbages?

RIGSBY. Accountants – lawyers – doctors. What do they know about life – except what they've read in library books.

RUTH. I wouldn't say that exactly.

RIGSBY. Of course, they do have one advantage over me. Something I haven't got – that I'll never have now. And which you're rather short of...

RUTH. What's that?

RIGSBY. Youth, Miss Jones. Youth is not on our side.

RUTH. *(coldly)* A little more on my side than yours, Mr Rigsby.

RIGSBY. I gave my youth making the world safe for democracy.

RUTH. Yes, and I'm sure we all appreciate that, Mr Rigsby.

RIGSBY. Are you? People soon forget. There were no flags out when I came back. There were no banners across the road saying "Welcome Home". They hoped I wasn't coming.

RUTH. Oh, I'm sure that's not true.

RIGSBY. I spent my twenty-first birthday in a foxhole – up to my knees in mud.

RUTH. Yes, you did tell me...

RIGSBY. I'm going to open my shirt now, Miss Jones.

RUTH. *(alarmed)* Mr Rigsby –

RIGSBY. Not with any lascivious intent but to show you something.

(He opens shirt.)

See that scar? Shrapnel. If that was to move another half inch – I would have been the last casualty of World War Two.

RUTH. Then perhaps you shouldn't exert yourself, Mr Rigsby.

(She looks towards the door.)

I wonder where they've got to...

(He blows furtively in her ear. She looks back in surprise.)

RIGSBY. *Au contraire*, Miss Jones. When you've been through what I've been through – it changes you. You see things differently. It gives you a zest for life. After

Anzio every day's a bonus. I don't believe in wasting time...

(He sips his wine and looks decidedly groggy.)

RUTH. Neither do I, Mr Rigsby.

(She attempts to rise. He stays her.)

RIGSBY. Are you sure, Miss Jones? Aren't you wasting your time with these two? When you could be with someone of your own age and background...

RUTH. I simply don't meet people like that, Mr Rigsby.

RIGSBY. What?

RUTH. There was someone once. I was engaged but it didn't work out...

RIGSBY. I did hear about that. And it's made you bitter, hasn't it?

RUTH. Yes.

RIGSBY. I've never let that happen to me. I was never bitter – even though my marriage was doomed from the start.

RUTH. Then why did you go through with it?

RIGSBY. Why did Hitler invade Russia? It seemed a good idea at the time. He wasn't aware of the enormity of the undertaking until he was confronted by those vast arctic wastes. It was the same with me. But it's never made me bitter. I still believe in happiness. Drink up, Miss Jones.

(RUTH empties her glass. He replenishes it.)

You're nervous of me, aren't you, Miss Jones?

RUTH. Well, I've heard stories...

RIGSBY. What stories?

RUTH. That your wife left you – and there was violence...

RIGSBY. Not by me. (*Reflects*) I'll always remember our wedding day. She was a vision in white – clad entirely in parachute silk due to the shortage of clothing coupons. She floated down the aisle like a detached barrage balloon and I realised then and there that in 'for better or for worse', it was definitely going to be worse – and it would be me who'd need the parachute.

RUTH. You've also been in trouble with the police.

RIGSBY. A vile slander. I was on my way home one night – I'd been drinking, I admit. I saw this woman knocked off her bike. She hadn't got any lights but that wouldn't have mattered, the driver was pissed. She lay in the gutter motionless. I told the driver what I thought of him and went to ring for an ambulance. While I was in the phone box the driver got back in his car and drove off. I didn't even get his number.

RUTH. Well, at least you didn't pass by on the other side, Mr Rigsby.

RIGSBY. I haven't finished. As I came out of the phone box the woman got up, shook herself, and pedalled off like the wind. No-one could have caught her. When the police arrived I was the only one there...

RUTH. What happened?

RIGSBY. I was arrested for being drunk and disorderly. Story of my life. More wine...?

(*He looks deep into her eyes and pours. She covers the glass. The wine begins to run over her hand.*)

RUTH. Oh!

RIGSBY. Sorry, Miss Jones. Let me get a towel.

(*He staggers across the room and returns with a towel.*)

RUTH. Thank you. Now I really must...

RIGSBY. (*focusing desperately*) What about Rachmaninov, Miss Jones?

RUTH. (*stares*) Rachmaninov? I didn't know you liked classical music, Mr Rigsby.

RIGSBY. It's food and drink to me, Miss Jones.

(*He crosses to the record player.*)

Ah, yes – it's on the turntable.

(*He stands back.*)

Now where is it?

RUTH. What are you looking for, Mr Rigsby?

RIGSBY. The handle.

RUTH. It works by electricity.

RIGSBY. So it does – the modern type...

(He switches the player on. There is a terrible dirge-like sound. He stands back in admiration.)

Delightful. You can't beat Rachmaninov. You can almost hear the waves beating against the rocks.

RUTH. Mr Rigsby – it's on the wrong speed – it should be thirty-three.

RIGSBY. Oh, so it should – my error.

(He adjusts the speed and swallows another couple of pills observed by **RUTH.** *He sways back to the settee and sits heavily, causing* **RUTH** *to bounce upwards.)*

Let it flow over you, Miss Jones. That's the thing to do. Doesn't it make you want to throw caution to the wind?

*(***RUTH** *looks around for a means of escape. He blows in her ear. She turns to find him uncomfortably close.)*

RUTH. Is there a draught, Mr Rigsby?

RIGSBY. The wind's off the North Sea again...

(His voice is slurred.)

But let the wind blow where it will, Miss Jones – don't fight it.

RUTH. What are you suggesting?

RIGSBY. *(into her ear)* Honi soit qui mal y pense.

RUTH. Pardon?

RIGSBY. *(huskily)* Respondez si'l vous plait.

(His head is now resting on her shoulder. His eyes are closed in a dreamy smile.)

RUTH. Mr Rigsby, are you ill? Mr Rigsby...

(She edges out from under him. He falls forward onto the settee. She prods him with her finger. There is no response. She tiptoes to the door and looks back. **RIGSBY**

rolls off the settee and crashes onto the floor. He remains motionless. **RUTH** *exits.*)

(Lights fade.)

(Curtain.)

Scene Two

(Attic flat. The following evening. **PHILIP** *is preparing to go out.* **ALAN** *is watching him from behind a book. There is tension between them.)*

ALAN. Going out?

PHILIP. *(shortly)* Yes.

ALAN. So, it's just a twosome?

PHILIP. No – it's a threesome.

ALAN. Oh. That could be awkward.

PHILIP. It is.

ALAN. Well, if you need me –

PHILIP. I don't.

ALAN. Oh. *(pause)* Did she mention me at all?

PHILIP. Yes.

ALAN. What did she say?

PHILIP. Don't bring him.

ALAN. *(stares)* Why?

PHILIP. She thinks you're weird.

ALAN. She thinks *I'm* weird? I think she's weird.

PHILIP. Then you should have suited each other.

ALAN. She had no conversation.

PHILIP. Well, that shouldn't have been a problem. You had enough for all of us. You never stopped talking. And all those long words. They didn't know what you were talking about. I didn't know what you were talking about! You made them feel illiterate. What they actually said was don't bring Dictionary.

ALAN. Dictionary! They've never seen a dictionary. They could barely express themselves. Where did you find them?

PHILIP. I didn't choose them for their conversation. Do you always gabble like that when you're nervous?

ALAN. I wasn't nervous. I was cagey.

PHILIP. Cagey!

ALAN. I should have told you. I don't make a move on the first date.

PHILIP. You mean you get a second one? You do surprise me.

ALAN. There's more to a relationship than sex, Philip.

PHILIP. How would you know?

ALAN. Besides, I hadn't brought anything...

PHILIP. Oh, yes you had.

(PHILIP *leans forward and removes* ALAN*'s wallet.*)

It was in your wallet. It's been in your wallet for a year. It's your constant companion. It's been in there so long it's worn a groove in the leather. When you finally take it out it'll probably disintegrate. If you don't disintegrate first.

ALAN. Just because I'm choosy.

PHILIP. Meaning I'm not?

ALAN. I think we could have done better.

PHILIP. Oh, you do?

ALAN. They smoked – chewed gum – wore too much make-up – and they had arrows on their stockings – pointing upwards.

PHILIP. She would have been ideal.

ALAN. I don't think so.

PHILIP. For the first time.

ALAN. It wouldn't have been for the first time!

(ALAN *watches* PHILIP *for a moment.*)

Look, if it's made things difficult – I don't mind making up the numbers...

PHILIP. I've just told you –

ALAN. Just mention me. Say we were talking and I said how much I liked her.

PHILIP. But you don't.

ALAN. Just say it. Then I could bump into you somewhere. I mean, I don't mind helping ou ...

PHILIP. *(regards* **ALAN***)* No – I'm sorry.

ALAN. So I'm staying here. And what happens when Ruth comes up looking for you. What am I supposed to say?

PHILIP. I don't really care. It's gone on too long. I can't stay in one place. You're forgetting – I'm a hunter-gatherer. And where Ruth's concerned I've hunted and I've gathered. Now I must move on – instinctively – like the lion migrates across the Masai Mara.

ALAN. I don't think she'll see it like that.

PHILIP. No – perhaps not...

(He studies **ALAN.***)*

You could help me out there.

ALAN. What?

PHILIP. We could help each other.

ALAN. Don't start that again.

PHILIP. Ruth would be ideal. She's kind, gentle and loving. And, in spite of appearances, a woman of the world.

ALAN. No.

PHILIP. Why not?

ALAN. Because you're using me. Why don't you simply tell her?

PHILIP. *(hesitates)* And hurt her feelings? No, this would be the ideal solution. And it's a perfect opportunity. Rigsby's still in bed. *(accusingly)* Sleeping it off.

*(***ALAN*** considers this.)*

ALAN. She'd be offended.

PHILIP. No woman is ever offended by that – not from someone she likes. And she does like you.

ALAN. Does she?

PHILIP. And do you know what she'd like most? That she would be your first.

ALAN. She wouldn't!

PHILIP. You never forget your first. I remember mine vividly. She was standing in a clearing – just a simple loincloth and the beads I'd given her as a wedding gift. She was as nervous as a gazelle. The young breasts were rising and falling – and I could see her heart winking under her skin...

(ALAN is hooked in spite of himself.)

I shall never forget. They say that everything after the first time is a pale imitation. That we spend the rest of our lives pursuing that moment.

ALAN. Well, I'm not spending the rest of my life pursuing someone like Miss Jones.

PHILIP. Why not?

ALAN. Then there's Rigsby – he'll kill me if he finds out.

PHILIP. He's going to kill you anyway – when he gets out of bed.

ALAN. *(uneasily)* He took too many tablets.

PHILIP. Good. Then you've got tonight. *(considers)* Say you like your girls long and leggy with funny little mouths – she'll like that.

ALAN. No.

PHILIP. All you have to do is knock on the ceiling...

ALAN. No.

(ALAN follows PHILIP to the door.)

She's older than I am.

(PHILIP pauses by the door.)

PHILIP. We have a saying in my country. "To the starving man all bread is fresh."

(PHILIP exits. ALAN picks up his wallet, looks inside and then slips it back into his jacket. He crosses to the door and wedges a chair under the knob. He tests it then removes it. He turns to the wardrobe. Opens the door and makes space inside. He opens and closes the door ushering an imaginary person inside.)

(He draws a deep breath and stamps lightly three times on the floor. He checks his appearance in the mirror.

*Adopts a pose of studied nonchalance. He adopts several
poses facing the door. He hears a sound on the stair. He
stands languidly with one hand in his pocket as the door
opens.* RIGSBY *enters angrily.*)

ALAN. *(stares)* Rigsby! What's the matter?

RIGSBY. You ask me that after nearly poisoning me?

ALAN. You're exaggerating.

(*He backs away.*)

RIGSBY. Exaggerating! I was drugged to the eyeballs. I slept
for nearly twenty-four hours. I still can't feel my teeth.
And that's not all – when I woke up, do you know what
I found? My water had turned green.

ALAN. *(nervously)* Green?

RIGSBY. Bright green.

ALAN. It'll fade.

RIGSBY. I took those tablets to my doctor. He said they
were for women in early pregnancy! Do I look like a
woman in early pregnancy? I thought of taking you
before the medical council – and then I thought of
something infinitely more satisfying, like wiping the
floor with you.

ALAN. I was only trying to help.

RIGSBY. No, you weren't. I think it was sabotage. You've
always been jealous of me and Miss Jones. Never
leaving us alone for a minute. I know your game.
You and your erogenous zones. Was she going to be
another notch on the bedpost? Or is she already there?

(*He seizes* ALAN.)

ALAN. *(desperately)* No! That was all talk, Rigsby. It didn't
mean anything.

RIGSBY. *(hesitates)* All talk! What do you mean, all talk?
You're a member of the permissive society, aren't you?
You know where the erogenous zones are.

ALAN. I know where the Himalayas are but I've never been up them. It was all talk. You've had more experience than I have.

*(**RIGSBY** releases him.)*

RIGSBY. Then you haven't had much! *(pause)* You mean, there's been no sea breaking against rocks – no rockets launching into space – no trains hurtling through tunnels?

ALAN. No?

RIGSBY. Well, I must say, you've been a big disappointment. What a washout.

ALAN. I don't know what you're complaining about. I was a big disappointment before. I've always been a big disappointment to you.

RIGSBY. That's true.

*(**ALAN** takes books and puts them on the table.)*

ALAN. From now on I shall dedicate myself to my books. All this has been too much of a distraction. They say that on average men think about women every thirty seconds.

RIGSBY. Every thirty seconds? You mean including *Match of The Day*? All that?

ALAN. Yes.

RIGSBY. *(considers)* Seems about right.

ALAN. But not anymore. Have you thought what we could achieve if we spent that time studying? We'd have discovered a cure for the common cold – found a substitute for oil – even the secret of life itself.

RIGSBY. *(pause)* I thought that was the secret of life itself.

ALAN. No – one day we'll be able to produce it out of a test tube.

*(**RIGSBY** pauses by the door.)*

RIGSBY. Won't be as much fun though, will it?

*(**RIGSBY** exits. **ALAN** listens to him descending the stairs. A slow smile crosses his face. He sweeps the books off the*

*table. He stands and stamps savagely on the floor. He
crosses and listens at the door. He opens it.)*

*(RUTH enters. She has dressed with care and is wearing
more bangles and beads than ever.)*

RUTH. Where is he?

ALAN. Philip's gone out.

RUTH. I thought I heard him knock.

ALAN. No, that was me.

*(He casually wedges a chair against the door. RUTH
watches him.)*

You know, we really should have a key to this door...

RUTH. *(quietly)* Is that important at the moment?

ALAN. It could be. Come and sit down.

(She joins ALAN on the settee and watches him curiously.)

Did I ever tell you that I like my girls long and leggy
with funny little mouths?

RUTH. No.

ALAN. Who does that remind you of?

RUTH. I've no idea.

*(The bangles become slightly agitated and she pushes
them up her arms.)*

ALAN. Are you sure, Ruth?

(He glances at the door.)

Excuse me.

*(He rises and picks up the table and places it against the
door alongside the chair. RUTH's eyes widen slightly. He
returns.)*

ALAN. Can't you guess?

(RUTH lowers her eyes.)

RUTH. Do you mean me?

ALAN. I've always been attracted to you – ever since that
first night on the bed.

(He takes his wallet from his jacket pocket and lays it significantly on the table. She regards it for a moment.)

RUTH. You're very young.

ALAN. That only means I've more to give. I'm not used up like that poor wretch down there. I'm not cynical like Philip.

(He begins to play with her bangles, sliding them up and down her arms.)

I wouldn't treat you like he does.

(He turns his attention to her beads twisting them round his fingers.)

I think of you all the time. I'm neglecting my work.

RUTH. You mustn't.

ALAN. That's easy to say. I shall probably fail. And it'll be your fault.

RUTH. Don't say that.

ALAN. I'm not well. The doctor's concerned. He can't understand what's wrong with me. I could tell him but I daren't. It's you. You're what's wrong with me. And you could cure me…

(He pulls her towards him and kisses her.)

Excuse me.

(She watches him as he takes a chest of drawers and places it on the table.)

RUTH. Are you going to move all the furniture?

ALAN. Don't laugh at me, Ruth.

(RUTH stands.)

RUTH. I'm not laughing, Alan. And it would be untrue to say I didn't know you were attracted to me. A woman can sense these things. I could feel you watching me. Looks can be a curse, Alan. I didn't mean to torment you. Oh, I may have encouraged you a little – flashed you a smile – left my hand on your arm a little too long. There's a little of the coquette in all of us. But

I didn't mean to unleash feelings and passions that can't be controlled...

(She's fully into her stride, flourishing her beads and bangles as she moves around the room.)

I knew this wasn't going to be an ordinary evening when the furniture began to pile against the door. Tell me – is it to stop people entering or to stop me leaving? Am I your prisoner?

ALAN. *(alarmed)* No. You can leave anytime.

RUTH. Oh. Then perhaps I should...

ALAN. Of course. I don't know what came over me. I've been working too hard. I'm running on empty. Please forget it.

(ALAN begins to remove the furniture.)

RUTH. But I can't forget it. Why, Alan? Why were you attracted to me? Because I was unattainable?

ALAN. *(struggling with furniture)* Sort of.

RUTH. Well, I'm not. I'm a woman. The eternal woman – with all her weakness and her mystery...

(ALAN has almost completed his furniture moving.)

But what happens when I'm no longer a mystery? What then? Will you despise me? Will I be just another conquest?

ALAN. I won't despise you. And you won't be another conquest. There hasn't been any conquests.

RUTH. *(stares)* You don't mean...? Alan, that's an incredible compliment.

(She kisses him. He begins to return the furniture to the door.)

But can I do this to you? Take your innocence?

ALAN. Yes, I don't want it.

(He returns more furniture.)

RUTH. But aren't we forgetting someone?

ALAN. Rigsby won't be back tonight.

RUTH. I meant Philip. Can we do this to him? He's your friend. I know how much that means to you. You worship him. You can't do this, Alan.

(ALAN sighs and begins to remove the furniture.)

ALAN. *(grumpily)* All right. But he's doing it to you.

RUTH. *(stares)* What?

ALAN. He's with a girl at this very moment. Her name's Sharon. She has arrows on her stockings.

RUTH. Arrows?

ALAN. And this was his idea.

RUTH. What?

ALAN. Well, in as much as it was mine. He said he wouldn't stand in our way.

RUTH. *(shocked)* He said that?

ALAN. Yes.

(RUTH turns away and sobs.)

Don't cry. He didn't mean to hurt you. He's not like us. He's a restless spirit. Nomadic. A hunter-gatherer. He moves by instinct. Like the animals that cross the Masai Mara in search of fresh pasture...

(RUTH turns.)

RUTH. You don't believe all that nonsense. He's never been to Africa. He comes from Croydon.

ALAN. Croydon!

RUTH. He's not a noble savage. I've seen his records.

ALAN. You mean he hasn't wrestled with crocodiles?

RUTH. Not in Croydon. Nor does he have ten wives.

ALAN. *(stares)* But you never said anything.

RUTH. *(shrugs)* It seemed to amuse him. He likes making fun of you. It seemed harmless. But he must have known I'd find out.

ALAN. So he's been making a fool of me all along.

(He returns to removing the furniture.)

RUTH. Yes. He said you'd believe anything.

ALAN. He's right. I believed everything he said.

RUTH. So did I.

(She puts a hand on his arm and stops him. He watches her as she pushes the table back in front of the door.)

Well, don't just stand there. Give me a hand with the drawers.

ALAN. You mean–?

RUTH. You're not the only one he's made a fool of...

(She puts out her hand. ALAN becomes alarmed.)

ALAN. Ah. Yes. Wait a minute. I haven't got anything. It would mean slipping out. Perhaps I could find an all-night chemist...

RUTH. You're not going to start moving the furniture again? *(takes his hand)* There's nothing to be afraid of...

(She moves towards the bedroom.)

ALAN. No...

(He pushes another piece of furniture against the door and follows her. They lie down on the bed.)

RUTH. *(softly)* It's all perfectly natural...

ALAN. Yes. So I understand.

RUTH. So why be nervous?

ALAN. Right.

(They move into a deep embrace. Sounds on the landing. The door is pushed against the furniture. The pile of furniture begins to collapse but they are oblivious.)

(As the lights begin to fade the bed collapses.)

(Curtain.)

Scene Three

(Attic flat. The following evening. PHILIP *is reading.)*

*(*ALAN *has finished packing a case in the bedroom. He carries it into the living room.* PHILIP *looks up.)*

PHILIP. Going home?

ALAN. No. I'm leaving.

PHILIP. *(surprised)* Leaving?

ALAN. I've found somewhere else.

PHILIP. I wondered where you'd been all day.

ALAN. *(hesitates)* I suppose I'd better tell Rigsby.

PHILIP. He's been drinking...

ALAN. Oh. Perhaps I'll leave a note.

PHILIP. Is that why you're leaving?

ALAN. What?

PHILIP. Because of Rigsby?

ALAN. No.

PHILIP. What happened last night?

ALAN. Nothing.

PHILIP. Then why are you leaving?

ALAN. I've found a better place...

(He crosses to the door and opens it. He sniffs.)

I can smell burning.

PHILIP. Yes. It's Rigsby. I gave him some love wood.

ALAN. What?

PHILIP. He's burning it outside Ruth's hut. The idea is she'll smell the smoke – come to the door – look deep into his eyes – and fall deeply in love with him.

ALAN. *(coldly)* Love wood. Do you think it'll work?

PHILIP. I doubt it. It came off the wardrobe.

ALAN. I thought so. Don't you ever get tired of this?

PHILIP. Tired of what?

ALAN. This pretence. You're not the son of a chief. You've never been to Africa. You haven't crossed the Serengeti – or climbed the peaks of Kilamanjaro. You come from Croydon!

PHILIP. She told you.

ALAN. Yes.

PHILIP. I thought she'd find out.

ALAN. She saw your records.

PHILIP. *(pause)* Terrible things...records.

ALAN. Is that all you can say?

PHILIP. Why did she tell you?

ALAN. I don't know. She just did.

PHILIP. After all this time? I find that strange. What happened?

ALAN. Nothing.

PHILIP. What did you tell her?

ALAN. Look, I don't know why I'm defending myself. This is all your fault. You threw us together.

PHILIP. Ah. So that's what happened.

ALAN. No.

PHILIP. And you spilled the beans – as they say in this country. *(pause)* I'll have to stop saying that.

ALAN. If you can – which I doubt.

PHILIP. Where are you going?

ALAN. The Cedars. It's nearer to college.

PHILIP. The Cedars. You were lucky to get in there.

ALAN. He's a friend of my father's. They know each other through the church.

PHILIP. Ah. Back to the safety of the church. Are you going to say goodbye to Ruth?

ALAN. No. Perhaps you could say goodbye for me.

PHILIP. Why should I?

ALAN. You're to blame for all this. You made fools of us. You said you were the son of a chief and we believed you.

PHILIP. You wanted to believe me.

(He looks around.)

At least I'll have more room.

ALAN. It was always too small...

(He picks up his case and opens the door. Closes it abruptly.)

Ruth's coming up!

(He pushes the suitcase out of sight. **RUTH** *backs into the room.)*

RUTH. Can you smell burning?

*(***PHILIP*** *and* **ALAN** *exchange glances.)*

PHILIP. Yes. Have you seen Rigsby?

RUTH. No. He's been drinking and hanging about outside my room. I waited until he went for a refill and came up here.

ALAN. He's burning love wood.

RUTH. What?

ALAN. You're supposed to smell the smoke and fall in love with him. Another one of Philip's stories.

PHILIP. *(shrugs)* You liked them once.

ALAN. When I thought they were true.

RUTH. It's time for a little honesty, Philip.

ALAN. Right.

RUTH. Have you told him?

ALAN. *(stares)* What?

RUTH. About us.

ALAN. *(hesitates)* Well, not exactly... *(pause)* Told him what?

RUTH. Last night, Philip – something happened. Something that may hurt you deeply. It was wild and unpredictable. We didn't plan it. A spark became a flame – a flame became a fire. Alan and I don't want our relationship to be founded on deceit. Last night Alan and I became lovers.

ALAN. What!

PHILIP. *(smiles)* I understand, Ruth. These things happen.

RUTH. Thank you, Philip. That must have cost you a great deal. I know everything's against us. I know what the world will say. I know what Alan's parents will say.

ALAN. *(alarmed)* My parents?

RUTH. That he's too young. That I'm too old. That it will never work. But we shall prove them wrong. *(stops)* What's this suitcase doing here?

PHILIP. It's Alan's.

ALAN. Yes. I've found another room. The Cedars. Just down the road. They've got central heating.

RUTH. *(stares)* Central heating?

ALAN. Yes.

RUTH. You were leaving for central heating?

ALAN. It's just down the road.

RUTH. You were leaving like a thief in the night – without saying a word. My God!

(The door opens. A piece of smoking wood appears. It is wafted around in the air. RUTH sniffs and turns. The wood is followed by RIGSBY, grinning insanely. He is holding a glass of beer in his other hand.)

RIGSBY. Over here, Miss Jones.

(He advances on her and wafts the smoke about her with little darting motions.)

RUTH. What are you doing, Mr Rigsby? You'll start a fire.

RIGSBY. I'll start a fire all right. Inhale, Miss Jones. You're not taking it down.

RUTH. It's choking me.

RIGSBY. It's love wood. It'll start a fire you'll never put out.

(RUTH finds she can retreat no further.)

RUTH. We'll see should we?

(She takes the glass from **RIGSBY**'s *hand and pours the beer over him and the wood.* **RIGSBY** *stares at the wood, drenched and bemused.)*

RIGSBY. It didn't work.

RUTH. Of course it didn't work. Because it's another one of Philips stories. It's not love wood. He hasn't got ten wives. He doesn't come from Africa. He comes from Croydon.

RIGSBY. Croydon! A southerner! I should have known. You can't trust them.

RUTH. You certainly can't trust Philip. He schemed to get me. Then he schemed for Alan to get me. Now he's scheming for you.

RIGSBY. What?

RUTH. As far as he's concerned it's any more for the Skylark, isn't it, Philip?

RIGSBY. *(louder)* What!

RUTH. *(sobs)* You men – you disgust me. You always want what you can't have – and when you have it, you don't want it. Always looking for your ideal and then destroying it – and then wishing for it. You're like men who shoot pheasants and then complain when they're scarce!

ALAN. Ruth, I didn't mean to hurt you –

(She turns on him savagely.)

RUTH. You were the worst. Judas. You betrayed me with a kiss.

RIGSBY. *(full volume)* What!

RUTH. You think you can just walk away? Something happened last night that shouldn't have happened, and now if something doesn't happen that should happen, what happens?

ALAN. *(hopefully)* I'll be just down the road...

RUTH. Have you any idea how pathetic that sounds? I trusted you – and you betrayed me.

RIGSBY. What?

(She crosses to the door, now thoroughly enjoying the scene. She turns dramatically, choking back a sob.)

Betrayed!

(They all start. She exits slamming the door behind her. Voice off.)

Betrayed!

(They listen to her descending the stairs.)

RUTH. *(from far off)* Betrayed!

(Her door slams. They start nervously again. PHILIP crosses and hands RIGSBY a towel. ALAN picks up his case. He starts to cross to the door.)

RIGSBY. Where are you going?

ALAN. To the Cedars.

RIGSBY. The Cedars?

ALAN. I've got a room there.

RIGSBY. They're Methodist.

ALAN. It was my father's idea. He thought I'd be more at home there.

RIGSBY. That's true. They're all sex mad.

ALAN. No, they're not.

RIGSBY. Yes, they are. Out to Sunday service then across the road to the newsagent for a copy of the News of the World. I've seen them.

*(**RIGSBY** takes **ALAN** by the shoulder as he edges towards the door.)*

There'll be no question of a refund of rent.

ALAN. I know.

RIGSBY. And I shall retain your deposit against damage.

ALAN. I haven't damaged anything.

RIGSBY. That bed will never be the same – and there's repairs to the floor – and there's damage to furniture.

Let's face it – you're a bloody vandal. I was going to give you notice anyway.

ALAN. Keep the deposit – it'll be worth it to get out of here.

(He pauses by the door. He looks back at PHILIP.)

I'll miss our talks.

PHILIP. Yes.

(ALAN exits.)

RIGSBY. Well that was a revelation. You're well rid of him.

PHILIP. Am I?

RIGSBY. I know the sort. Always trying to find someone to look up to... If it wasn't you – it was me.

PHILIP. *(smiles)* You think so?

RIGSBY. Yes. His trouble was he had a bad case of hero worship. And the trouble with that sort is – they're always going to be disappointed – then we get the looks of reproach...

PHILIP. I know.

RIGSBY. So you haven't got ten wives – and this is isn't love wood?

PHILIP. No – it came off the wardrobe.

RIGSBY. *(erupts)* What!

(He crosses to check the wardrobe.)

You mean I'm burning my own wardrobe? Haven't you any respect for other people's property? You're going through this place like a whirling Dervish.

(He stops and looks down at the wood.)

I didn't really believe it. I thought it was worth a try.

PHILIP. It's always worth a try, Rigsby.

RIGSBY. So you're not even married?

PHILIP. No.

RIGSBY. You're lucky. Marry in haste – repent at leisure – that was me. One harmless remark. I didn't know she was going to turn homicidal with a bread knife. Couldn't relax after that. Every time she started cutting a loaf I was on the edge. Of course, that was before sliced bread.

PHILIP. Do you ever see her?

RIGSBY. No. We still celebrate our anniversary though, only I do it here and she does it in Manchester.

(He crosses to the door and listens.)

Is she crying?

PHILIP. I wouldn't be surprised.

RIGSBY. She'll be feeling lonely.

PHILIP. I suppose so.

RIGSBY. She's been trifled with.

PHILIP. Yes.

RIGSBY. I wouldn't have done that.

PHILIP. I know.

RIGSBY. Youth. Fancy preferring him when she could have had me.

PHILIP. Women have always been a bad judge of men.

RIGSBY. That's true. So you think I still have a chance?

PHILIP. Why not? A war hero.

RIGSBY. *(pause)* I'm not a war hero.

PHILIP. What?

RIGSBY. When that shell got the captain I never stopped running. I joined the 49th Deserters. Spent the last two years of the war in psychiatric. They'd have shot me in the first war. That's why there were no flags out when I came home. They don't say anything but they know. They don't look at me, the hood-eyed bastards. Why are you smiling?

PHILIP. Well, neither of us are what we seem.

RIGSBY. What do you mean?

PHILIP. I come from Croydon.

(RIGSBY studies him.)

RIGSBY. You didn't get that tan in Croydon. That's an African tan.

PHILIP. Rigsby, I was born in Croydon.

RIGSBY. That doesn't make you Croydon. If a cat gives birth in a banana box what would you expect to find? Kittens or bananas?

PHILIP. *(stares)* Kittens.

RIGSBY. That's my point. And how do we know you're not the son of a chief? You look like the son of a chief. Your ancestor could have been out picking mangoes one morning and been confronted by a large gent in a fez and his mates. The next day he was on a sea trip to the West Indies – all expenses paid.

PHILIP. *(smiles)* I suppose you could be right.

RIGSBY. Come to that – how do we know this isn't love wood?

PHILIP. It came off the wardrobe.

RIGSBY. And do you know what that wardrobe's made of? African mahogany. We may have shaped it – and put a veneer on it – but it grew in Africa. It could be love wood.

PHILIP. But it didn't work.

RIGSBY. She didn't believe. You've got to believe in it.

(He crosses to the door.)

Do you think I should go to her?

PHILIP. Not at the moment.

RIGSBY. What would you do?

PHILIP. Well, in my country... *(stops)*

RIGSBY. No – go on.

*(He crosses back to **PHILIP**.)*

PHILIP. We'd wait for a full moon.

RIGSBY. Yes, that's a powerful force, isn't it?

PHILIP. It can draw the seas to it, Rigsby. Animals won't sleep in its rays lest it drives them mad. Birds believe it's day and thrash their wings...All nature becomes restless...Men become silver in the night...And women wait...

(Their heads are now very close together. **PHILIP** *'s voice becomes lower and lower. There is the sound of drums and African chanting.)*

(The lights fade)

(Curtain.)

The End.

MUSIC USE NOTE

Licensees are solely responsible for obtaining formal written permission from copyright owners to use copyrighted music in the performance of this play and are strongly cautioned to do so. If no such permission is obtained by the licensee, then the licensee must use only original music that the licensee owns and controls. Licensees are solely responsible and liable for all music clearances and shall indemnify the copyright owners of the play(s) and their licensing agent, Samuel French, against any costs, expenses, losses and liabilities arising from the use of music by licensees. Please contact the appropriate music licensing authority in your territory for the rights to any incidental music.

IMPORTANT BILLING AND CREDIT REQUIREMENTS

If you have obtained performance rights to this title, please refer to your licensing agreement for important billing and credit requirements.

CPSIA information can be obtained
at www.ICGtesting.com
Printed in the USA
BVHW041151110821
614199BV00012B/136

9 780573 113765